D1520364

DIEGO RIVERA

Recent Titles in Greenwood Biographies

Frederick Douglass: A Biography
C. James Trotman

Sojourner Truth: A Biography
Larry G. Murphy

Harriet Tubman: A Biography
James A. McGowan and William C. Kashatus

George Washington Carver: A Biography
Gary R. Kremer

Lance Armstrong: A Biography
Paula Johanson

Prince William: A Biography
Joann F. Price

Oprah Winfrey: A Biography
Helen S. Garson

John F. Kennedy: A Biography
Michael Meagher and Larry D. Gragg

Maya Lin: A Biography
Donald Langmead

Stonewall Jackson: A Biography
Ethan S. Rafuse

Rosa Parks: A Biography
Joyce A. Hanson

Emiliano Zapata: A Biography
Albert Rolls

DIEGO RIVERA

A Biography

Manuel Aguilar-Moreno
and Erika Cabrera

GREENWOOD BIOGRAPHIES

AN IMPRINT OF ABC-CLIO, LLC
Santa Barbara, California • Denver, Colorado • Oxford, England

Library of Congress Cataloging-in-Publication Data

Aguilar-Moreno, Manuel.
Diego Rivera : a biography / Manuel Aguilar-Moreno and Erika Cabrera.
p. cm. — (Greenwood biographies)
Includes index.
ISBN 978-0-313-35406-9 (hardback) — ISBN 978-0-313-35407-6 (ebook) 1. Rivera, Diego, 1886-1957. 2. Painters—Mexico—Biography. I. Cabrera, Erika. II. Title.
ND259.R5A84 2011
759.972—dc23
[B] 2011023984

ISBN: 978-0-313-35406-9
EISBN: 978-0-313-35407-6

15 14 13 12 11 1 2 3 4 5

This book is also available on the World Wide Web as an eBook.
Visit www.abc-clio.com for details.

Greenwood
An Imprint of ABC-CLIO, LLC

ABC-CLIO, LLC
130 Cremona Drive, P.O. Box 1911
Santa Barbara, California 93116-1911

This book is printed on acid-free paper ∞

Manufactured in the United States of America

*To Diego Rivera, Frida Kahlo, and all artists who,
searching for the meaning of life, express their love,
sorrow, and truth through their art.*

CONTENTS

SERIES FOREWORD

In response to high school and public library needs, Greenwood developed this distinguished series of full-length biographies specifically for student use. Prepared by field experts and professionals, these engaging biographies are tailored for high school students who need challenging yet accessible biographies. Ideal for secondary school assignments, the length, format, and subject areas are designed to meet educators' requirements and students' interests.

Greenwood offers an extensive selection of biographies spanning all curriculum-related subject areas including social studies, the sciences, literature and the arts, history and politics, as well as popular culture, covering public figures and famous personalities from all time periods and backgrounds, both historic and contemporary, who have made an impact on American and/or world culture. Greenwood biographies were chosen based on comprehensive feedback from librarians and educators. Consideration was given to both curriculum relevance and inherent interest. The result is an intriguing mix of the well known and the unexpected, the saints and sinners from long-ago history and contemporary pop culture. Readers will find a wide array of subject choices from fascinating crime figures like Al Capone to inspiring pioneers like Margaret Mead, from the greatest minds of our time like Stephen Hawking to the most amazing success stories of our day like J.K. Rowling.

While the emphasis is on fact, not glorification, the books are meant to be fun to read. Each volume provides in-depth information about the subject's life from birth through childhood, the teen years, and adulthood. A thorough account relates family background and education, traces personal and professional influences, and explores struggles, accomplishments, and contributions. A timeline highlights the most significant life events against a historical perspective. Bibliographies supplement the reference value of each volume.

ACKNOWLEDGMENTS

Special thanks to Emily Birch, Wendi Schnaufer, Debby Adams, Tiffany Wayne, Kim Kennedy-White, Zaher Karp, and the editorial staff of ABC-CLIO for their enlightening support and orientation during the writing process of the book.

INTRODUCTION

In 1921, Mexico was recovering from a violent revolution that lasted 10 years and changed the course of the country forever. The minister of education, José Vasconcelos, had the challenge of dealing with a 90 percent illiteracy rate. He decided to launch a vigorous campaign of public education, which included a mural program developed in collaboration with artist Dr. Atl. This program had the purpose of educating the public about the history of Mexico and the sociopolitical ideas of the revolution. Artists like Dr. Atl, Roberto Montenegro, Xavier Guerrero, and Gabriel Fernández Ledesma participated in creating the first mural under this program in a former Jesuit school, El Colegio de San Pedro y San Pablo in Mexico City. This was the beginning of Mexican muralism, the first mural movement in the world since the Italian Renaissance. Murals became an accessible and public visual dialogue with the Mexican people, an effective way to represent popular culture and everyday life and to interact with cultural and religious traditions. Muralism was a reaction against the modern expression of the ego by the individual artists because the murals could not be bought or sold. The murals expressed the most significant epics of the national experience and were thought of as painted books at the service of common people, located in the main public buildings of Mexico. The protagonists of the murals were not the kings or legendary heroes of previous artistic traditions, but the very people themselves.

In June 1921, Diego Rivera, a Mexican artist who had been living and painting in Europe for 14 years, returned to Mexico. He was incorporated into the Vasconcelos mural program and, at the beginning of 1922, Rivera started his first mural, titled *The Creation*. Rivera reconnected with his own country, portraying the beauty and colors of its landscapes, the joy of its people, and the animation of its open-air markets. Had Rivera remained in Europe, without a doubt he would still be recognized as a great artist and his work would be exhibited in European museums. Returning to Mexico, however, Rivera became not only one of the most important artists of the muralist movement but one of the world's most renowned artists of the 20th century.

Rivera was a mythomaniac who created a legend of himself. His autobiography and other biographies describe extravagant stories about his hundreds of lovers, his meetings with Hitler and Stalin, his experience eating human flesh, and a host of other social and political scandals. His tumultuous relationship with artist Frida Kahlo added controversy to his already agitated life. The chaos of his life story presents a person and an artist who had many faces: the Union Leader, the Storyteller, the Marxist Revolutionary, the Archaeologist, the Bohemian, the Womanizer, the Egoist, and the Charmer. All of those characteristics may be true in some sense, but emerging from the stories and controversy is the career of a dedicated and unique artist, a talented, creative, passionate, and prolific painter with a capacity to work 18 hours a day, who through his art dignified the values of the Mexican Indians and offered a strong social and political criticism of history and his own times.

Diego Rivera emerges larger than life itself and, in spite of the contradictions of his own controversial persona, is remembered as one of the most gifted artists of the 20th century. Rivera became for Mexico what Pablo Picasso is for Spain or Andy Warhol is for the United States.

Diego Rivera has come, in some sense, to represent the very essence and identity of 20th-century Mexico.

TIMELINE: EVENTS IN THE LIFE OF DIEGO RIVERA

1861 Benito Juárez is elected president of Mexico.

1867 Benito Juárez defeats the French and overthrows the Emperor Maximilian of Habsburg. Juárez returns to the presidency and stays until 1872.

1876 General Porfirio Díaz seizes the presidency from Juárez. Díaz remains president almost continuously until 1911, a period known as the *Porfiriato*.

1886 José Diego María Rivera and his twin brother José Carlos María Rivera are born on December 8 in the city of Guanajuato, Mexico.

1888 Diego's twin brother, Carlos, dies at the age of one and a half.

Diego moves to the countryside to live with his nanny Antonia until the age of four.

1889 At the age of three, Diego Rivera begins to draw.

1891 Diego's sister María is born.

1892 The Rivera family moves to Mexico City.

1896 Diego Rivera attends a night course at the Academy of San Carlos at the age of 10.

1897 Rivera receives a scholarship that enables him to attend the Academy of San Carlos full time. While there, he studies with Félix Parra, José María Velasco, and Santiago Rebull and meets the famous engraver José Guadalupe Posada.

1902 Rivera receives a scholarship from Governor Teodoro A. Dehesa.

1903 Rivera joins *Grupo Bohemio*, led by Dr. Atl.

1904 Rivera enrolls in a course of anatomy at the medical school in Mexico City.

1905 Rivera is expelled from the Academy of San Carlos in reaction to demonstrations he leads that turn into riots.

1906 Rivera joins *Savia Moderna*, a group of artists, architects, and writers who create a magazine.
Rivera receives financial help from Governor Dehesa to travel to Europe with the condition that Rivera puts on a one-man show at the Academy of San Carlos, at which Rivera exhibits 26 works.

1907–1908 Rivera lives and travels in Spain.
Rivera lives with Eduardo Chicharro and becomes his disciple.

1909 Rivera travels throughout Europe.
Rivera moves to Paris and attends free lectures at the Academy of Montparnasse.
Rivera travels to Bruges (Belgium) to paint and meets Russian artist Angeline Beloff.

1910 Rivera exhibits at the Society of Independent Artists in Paris.
Rivera returns to Mexico to exhibit at the Academy of San Carlos.
The Mexican Revolution begins.
The Centro Artístico is established in Mexico City.

1911 Rivera returns to Paris and lives with Beloff, now considered his wife.
Revolutionaries Pancho Villa and Emiliano Zapata begin to fight in the north and south of Mexico.

	Rivera is apparently involved in an unsuccessful plot to assassinate President Díaz, who is forced into exile.
	In June, Rivera returns to Europe to work on a new Paris exhibit.
1913	Rivera begins his cubist period and exhibits in Salon d'Automne with the painting titled *Retrato de Adolfo Best Maugard*.
	When President Madero is assassinated, Rivera loses his financial aid from the Mexican government.
	Rivera meets Pablo Picasso.
1914	Rivera holds a solo exhibit at the Berthe Weill gallery in Paris.
1914–1918	World War I. Rivera travels in Spain.
1915	Rivera and Picasso have a falling-out over the painting titled *Paisaje Zapatista-La Guerrilla*.
1916	Rivera exhibits at Modern Gallery in New York.
	In August, Angeline Beloff gives birth to a son, Diego Rivera Jr.
	Rivera begins relationship with Russian artist Marevna Vorobiev-Stebelska.
	Rivera gives up cubism and is influenced by the impressionism of Cezanne and others.
1917	Diego Rivera Jr. becomes ill and dies in October at age 14 months.
1919	In November, Vorobiev-Stebelska gives birth to a daughter, Marika Rivera.
1920	Rivera travels to Italy to study fresco painting.
	José Vasconcelos is appointed secretary of education in Mexico under the presidency of Alvaro Obregón.
1921	Rivera leaves Paris and returns to Mexico.
1922	Vasconcelos commissions Rivera to paint in the Bolívar Amphitheatre in the School of San Ildefonso (National Preparatory School).
	Rivera begins to paint his first mural, *Creation*, in the National Preparatory School.
	Rivera marries Guadalupe Marín.

Rivera helps found the Sindicato Revolucionario de Obreros Técnicos y Plásticos (Revolutionary Union of Technical Workers, Painters, Sculptors, and Allied Trades) as a community of artists with a common goal to perpetuate socialistic ideas through art and muralism.

Rivera joins the Mexican Communist Party.

1923 Inauguration of the *Creation* mural.

Rivera begins his second group of murals in the Ministry of Education, the *Courtyard of Labor* and *Courtyard of Fiestas*.

1924 Rivera begins work on the mural at the National Agricultural School at Chapingo.

Lupe Marín gives birth to a daughter, Guadalupe.

1925 Rivera resigns from the Communist Party, but is readmitted the following year.

1927 Lupe Marín gives birth to a second daughter, Ruth; several months later, Marín and Rivera separate.

Rivera is invited by the Russian People's Commissar of Education, Anatoly Lunacharsky, to visit the Soviet Union.

1928 German author and friend Lotte Schwartz publishes the book *Das Werk Diego Riveras*.

Rivera is commissioned to design the scenes, props, and costumes for a ballet titled *H.P.* (*Horse Power*).

Rivera meets Frida Kahlo at a party hosted by photographer Tina Modotti.

1929 In August, Rivera and Kahlo are married.

Rivera begins to paint the mural titled *The History of Mexico* in the National Palace of Mexico City.

Rivera is commissioned by the American ambassador to Mexico, Dwight Morrow, to paint a mural at the Cortés Palace in the city of Cuernavaca.

1930 Rivera and Kahlo arrive in San Francisco where Rivera is to paint a mural titled *The Allegory of California* for the Stock Exchange.

1931 Rivera begins to paint the mural titled *The Making of a Fresco* in the California School of Fine Arts (San Francisco Art Institute).
Rivera and Kahlo return to Mexico to continue the mural at the National Palace.
Rivera, Kahlo, and the art dealer Frances Flynn Paine sail to New York for Rivera's solo exhibition at the New York Museum of Modern Art.

1932 Rivera and Kahlo arrive in Detroit to begin a mural at the Detroit Institute of Art.
Kahlo suffers a miscarriage and stays at the Henry Ford Hospital.
Rivera is commissioned to paint at the RCA building of the Rockefeller Center.

1933 Rivera submits designs for the RCA mural titled *Man at the Crossroads*; the mural is subsequently suspended as a result of controversy over inclusion of a portrait of Vladimir Lenin.
Rivera paints a series of portable panels titled *Portrait of America* at the New Workers' School in New York.
Rivera and Kahlo sail to Mexico in December.

1934 The RCA mural in New York is destroyed; Rivera subsequently signs a contract to paint a copy of the RCA mural at the Palacio de Bellas Artes in Mexico City.
The League of Revolutionary Artists and Writers (LEAR) is created in Mexico City with Rivera as advisor.
Rivera and Bertram Wolfe collaborate on a book about the murals, also titled *Portrait of America*.
Rivera has an affair with Frida Kahlo's younger sister, Cristina Kahlo.
Lázaro Cárdenas becomes president of Mexico.

1935 Rivera and Kahlo temporarily separate.
Rivera and Siqueiros, Mexican revolutionary artist, get into a fight brandishing pistols.

Rivera completes murals at the National Palace.

Alberto Misrachi becomes Rivera's art dealer.

1936 Rivera is hospitalized for an eye and kidney infection.

Rivera is commissioned to paint a mural at the Hotel Reforma; his frescoes are not installed because they contain negative portrayals of Mexican political figures.

Rivera joins the Trotskyite International Communist League and persuades President Cárdenas to grant Trotsky political asylum in Mexico.

1937 Leon and Natalia Trotsky arrive in Mexico and stay with Rivera and Kahlo at their house in the district of Coyoacan.

1938 Surrealists André and Jacqueline Breton arrive in Mexico and spend time with Rivera, Kahlo, and the Trotskys.

Kahlo travels to New York and Paris for her first art exhibitions.

1939 Rivera's friendship with Trotsky ends after Rivera discovers Kahlo's affairs with Trotsky and others; Rivera and Kahlo separate again and later divorce.

Rivera begins a series of paintings of the dancer Modelle Boss and the actress Paulette Goddard.

1940 Rivera participates in the "Exposición Internacional del Surrealismo" (International Exhibition of Surrealism) in the Galería de Arte Mexicano in Mexico City.

Rivera paints a mural, *Pan-American Unity*, for the Art in Action program of the Golden Gate International Exposition in San Francisco.

Rivera exhibits at the San Francisco Museum of Art.

In August, Leon Trotsky is assassinated in Mexico.

Kahlo arrives in San Francisco to reconcile with Rivera and they are remarried.

General Manuel Avila Camacho becomes president of Mexico.

1942 Rivera begins a series of panels on the pre-Conquest cultures for the second floor corridor at the Palacio Nacional in Mexico City.

Rivera begins construction of his home and museum compound, Anahuacalli.

1943 Rivera paints two murals at the National Institute of Cardiology in Mexico City.
Rivera becomes a member of the Colegio Nacional (National Academy) as a representative of the plastic arts.

1944 Rivera begins a mosaic decoration at Anahuacalli.

1945 Rivera paints *The Great City of Tenochtitlán* in the National Palace.

1946 Miguel Alemán becomes president of Mexico.
Emma Hurtado becomes Rivera's art dealer.

1947 Rivera is admitted into the American British Hospital in Mexico City to treat his bronchial pneumonia.
Rivera begins the *Dream of a Sunday Afternoon in the Alameda* mural in Hotel del Prado.
Rivera cofounds the National Institute of Fine Arts Commission for Mural Painting (INBA).

1948 Rivera finishes the Hotel del Prado mural, but part of it is concealed from public viewing to obscure controversial statements within the painting.
Rivera returns to Chapingo to add images of President Manuel Avila Camacho and Alvaro Obregón.

1949 Frida Kahlo is accepted into the Communist Party.
Rivera holds a major retrospective of his work, *Diego Rivera: 50 Años de su Labor Artistica*, at the Palacio de Bellas Artes.

1950 Kahlo has a spinal operation.
Rivera completes the murals at the Palacio Nacional titled *The Totonac Civilization* and *The Huastec Civilization*.
Rivera illustrates Pablo Neruda's *Canto General*.
The Mexican government awards Rivera the National Art Prize.
Rivera campaigns for the antinuclear Stockholm Peace Conference.

1951 Rivera holds a retrospective exhibition at the Houston Museum of Fine Arts.
Rivera paints underwater murals at the Lerma Waterworks in Mexico City.

1952 Rivera is commissioned by the INBA to paint a mural for an exhibition titled "Mexican Art from Pre-Columbian Times to the Present," but the director refuses to exhibit the work titled *The Nightmare of War and the Dream of Peace* upon viewing its controversial content; the rejected painting is returned to Rivera, who later displays the work in Paris.
Rivera meets American architect Frank Lloyd Wright.

1953 José María Dávila commissions Rivera to create a glass mosaic mural for the Teatro de los Insurgentes.
Rivera begins mural at the Hospital de la Raza titled *The People's Demand for Better Health*.
Rivera sends *The Nightmare of War and the Dream of Peace* to the People's Republic of China.
Kahlo's right leg is amputated below the knee to treat gangrene.

1954 Rivera and Kahlo participate in a public demonstration against the U.S. Central Intelligence Agency involvement in the coup d'etat against Guatemalan president Jacobo Arbenz.
Frida Kahlo dies on July 13.

1955 Rivera is diagnosed with a recurrence of cancer first detected a few years earlier.
Rivera marries his art dealer, Emma Hurtado, and the two travel to Moscow, where Rivera undergoes experimental cancer treatment.
Rivera sets up a trust fund through Banco de México to administer Anahuacalli and Kahlo's Coyoacan home museum.

1956 Rivera and Hurtado travel to Prague, Poland, and East Germany.
Rivera paints *Parade in Moscow*
Rivera announces he is Catholic.

1957 Rivera decorates the Mexico City residence of Dolores Olmedo in mosaic.

Rivera suffers a blood clot and phlebitis which causes his right arm to become paralyzed; he continues to try to paint.

Diego Rivera dies of heart failure in his San Angel studio on November 24; he is buried in the Rotonda de los Hombres Ilustres at the Panteón de Dolores in Mexico City.

Chapter 1

CHILDHOOD AND ARTISTIC FORMATION (1886–1906)

> Finding myself in art was to be a long and painful process. Looking back upon my work, I think the best I have done grew out of things deeply felt, the worst from a pride in mere talent.[1]

The Rivera family lived in the picturesque Mexican town of Guanajuato on 80 Pocitos Street. The future artist and muralist Diego Rivera was born there on December 8, 1886. Rivera in his later memoirs referred to this house as "the house of my parents . . . that small marble palace." Both of Rivera's parents, Diego Rivera Sr. and María Barrientos, came from a line of European ancestors who settled in the state of Guanajuato, Mexico. Rivera descended from the intermixing of diverse ethnicities such as Spanish, Russian, Italian, Portuguese, Native American, Jewish, and African. Rivera's ancestors were politically involved men and women who used their talents to participate in the development of Mexico.

According to his own account, Rivera's maternal grandfather, Juan Barrientos, was a mine operator from Veracruz who was of black descent and his maternal grandmother, Nemesia Rodríguez Valpuesta, was of Indian and Spanish mixture. After Nemesia became a widow, she was the owner of a school in Guanajuato where her daughters, including Diego's mother, María, were teachers. According to Rivera, Feliciano Rodriguez, Nemesia's brother, formed part of Emperor Maximilian's army during the French intervention, and he had a child with Empress Carlota, who later would become the famous General Maxime Weygand. Rivera recounts that in 1918 during a stay in the town of Perigueux, France, in the company of Dr. Elie Faure, a distinguished French art historian, he had a casual and emotional meeting with General Weygand. The General said, "My little Diego! . . . Come and give me a hug! How is my cousin, your mother?" Unfortunately there were no witnesses to corroborate this story, and it may be that Rivera's claim to European nobility was merely an attempt to claim a diverse and prestigious background.

Diego Rivera's paternal grandfather, Don Anastasio de Rivera, lived in Spain but was born in Russia. He was the son of an Italian mercenary who had served in the Spanish military and was on a diplomatic mission in Russia when Anastasio was born. Like his father, Don Anastasio de Rivera was an officer in the Spanish army and at some point he decided to emigrate to Mexico. He established himself in Guanajuato where he bought a mine and enjoyed some prosperity, until the mine was flooded and he was financially ruined. Don Anastasio married Inés Acosta y Peredo, a beautiful Mexican girl who descended from a Portuguese-Jewish family. Don Anastasio was married at the age of 50 and Inés was only 17, but Rivera reported that his grandfather "was a man of fabulous vigour" and they had nine children.[2] The eldest one was Diego Rivera Acosta, the artist's father. At the age of 65, Don Anastasio joined Benito Juárez in the war against the French and the persecution of the Catholic Church. It is believed that Don Anastasio died in that war.

Benito Juárez was an indigenous leader who fought for the defense of the Mexican Federal Republic and civil rights of the marginalized citizens. Juárez was elected president in 1861 after a long and treacherous civil war between his liberal party and the opposing conservative party. He established a reform to separate state from church. A few years later, France invaded Mexico and instituted Habsburg rule under

Prince Maximilian. Juárez and his fellow liberals fought with great valor and then drove the French and conservative bureaucracy out of power in 1867. Juárez has been remembered as a progressive reformist who fought for the consolidation of the Mexican Republic and the rights of the Mexican indigenous people. Juárez also established a nationwide educational system for all the citizens of Mexico.

Juárez ruled for a second time between 1867 and 1872, when he died in office. He was succeeded by Sebastián Lerdo de Tejada, who ruled until 1876. When Lerdo de Tejada tried to seek reelection, General Porfirio Díaz organized the Plan of Tuxtepec in order to overthrow President Lerdo. New elections were instituted and Porfirio Díaz, a charismatic military hero during the war against the French, was elected president. He established a dictatorship that ran from 1876 to 1910 until he was overthrown by the Mexican Revolution. President Díaz's government, although controversial, brought Mexico into modernity. Díaz brought about material progress in many areas, but because of the uneven distribution of resources, social inequalities alienated poor peasants and workers. As a consequence, a violent revolution erupted, with the goal to stop Díaz's dictatorial powers and to establish democracy and attempt the redemption of the underprivileged classes. During this time, which was known as the Porfiriato period, Rivera Sr. would live most of his adulthood. Don Anastasio would also teach his son Rivera Sr. certain ideological principles that eventually would transform the life of his son, the artist.

At the age of 13, Rivera Sr. enlisted in the war between Mexico and the French invaders. He served in the army for seven years, leaving in 1869 with the rank of major. Once he returned to Guanajuato, he became a schoolteacher and then an inspector of rural schools for the state of Guanajuato. Despite his government job, Rivera Sr. was active in voicing his political and social opinions. He was a Freemason and a liberal activist who believed that there should be a separation of state and church as well as equality for the working class. He was elected as a municipal councilman of Guanajuato, and he founded an *escuela normal* to train rural schoolteachers. In addition, Rivera Sr. edited a journal, *The Democrat,* through which he stated his beliefs about reform in Mexico. At the age of 34, Rivera Sr. married María del Pilar

Barrientos, also a schoolteacher, who was 15 years younger. By the age of 21, María Barrientos de Rivera had already had four pregnancies, but only one would come to full term.

On December 8, 1886, María Barrientos de Rivera gave birth to twin boys, who were named José Carlos María and José Diego María de la Concepción Juan Nepomuceno Estanislao de la Rivera y Barrientos Acosta y Rodríguez. During the delivery, María suffered a hemorrhage and lost such a large amount of blood that she entered into a deep coma, a state of catalepsy that the attending physician, Dr. Arizmendi, misdiagnosed as death. As María's sister, Cesárea, was preparing the body for the funeral, María's maid, known as old Martha, came to say farewell and kissed María on the forehead. Martha felt María breathe and began to cry, shouting that María was alive. Incredulous, Dr. Arizmendi performed the blister test: he held a lit match to María's skin and, to his surprise, a blister formed immediately, demonstrating that María Rivera was indeed alive. As these events happened on December 8, the day of the feast of the Virgin of the Dawn, the family interpreted it as a miraculous resurrection.[3]

At the age of one and a half, one of the brothers, José Carlos Rivera, died. In her grief, María Rivera began to visit the grave site of José Carlos every day and eventually fell into a deep depression. Out of desperation, the Rivera family encouraged María to study for a career. She eventually graduated with a diploma in obstetrics and began working in this field.

At the age of two, Diego began to show signs of fatigue and physical weakness, perhaps because he felt abandoned by his mother, who was so deeply affected by the death of José Carlos. To help cope with the death of his twin brother, Rivera's parents decided to send Diego with his Tarascan Indian nurse, Antonia, to her village in the mountainous countryside. Rivera later remembered that Antonia was a young woman in her mid-20s who had elegant, strong, and classic indigenous features. Rivera remembered Antonia as a healer and magician who allowed him to wander in the forest; there he played for hours among animals that included snakes and jaguars, who became his friends.[4] Rivera was surrounded by nature for the entire stay in the countryside, where he lived with Antonia for two years. By the time Rivera returned home, he was a healthy and chubby four-year-old. Throughout his life he expressed that he loved Antonia more than he did his own mother, who complained that Diego had become a "little Indian."

Diego Rivera grew up in a home that embraced two different sets of religious and political beliefs. Rivera Sr. was liberal and anticlerical, while his mother and aunts were strict traditional Catholics. In keeping with the antireligious ideology of Rivera Sr., the Rivera home never displayed the religious pictures or images that were typical of Catholic homes and Diego never stepped foot into a church until his Aunt Vicenta took him at the age of six. The young Rivera used his first visit to church as an opportunity to voice his own antireligious opinions of the clergy. He said, "On entering the Church, my repulsion was so great that I still get a sick feeling in my stomach when I recall it."[5]

As a young child Rivera had little to no religious teaching and his education was concentrated mostly in areas such as science and mathematics. Instead of teaching Diego about religion, Rivera Sr. focused on teaching him how to read. Diego Rivera learned how to read at the age of four and became an intelligent child.

Rivera also showed interest in art as a young child. At the age of three, Rivera began to draw. His parents made his first studio by draping black canvas on the walls and floor, where he basically made his first murals. Rivera showed a precocious attraction for mechanical devices and began to draw machines such as trains and locomotives, which were among his interests as a child. He was given the nickname "el ingeniero" (the engineer) because he enjoyed trains and mining machinery. There is a photograph that depicts Rivera at the age of four modeling with his favorite pastime hobby . . . trains. Rivera Sr. would often take Diego to the railroad depot, where he would watch the trains' arrival and departure.

At the age of six, Diego and the Rivera family moved to Mexico City. The decision was made when María, Rivera's mother, felt the family's security was being threatened by the increasing social inequalities that created despair among the urban poor and working classes. Rivera Sr. was among the educated liberals in Mexico who were active in fighting for the political and social rights of the working poor. Riots broke out in the city of Guanajuato, and Rivera Sr. protested in favor of the oppressed miners and peasants, which resulted in his gaining enemies among government officials. One day when he was away on business, María, scared of the increasing hostility that the conservative people of Guanajuato had toward her family, sold all of the family's belongings and took the children to Mexico City. A note from his wife explained to Rivera Sr. what had happened and he soon joined his family. In Mexico City, Rivera Sr. found a job as a clerk in the Department of Public Health while María worked as a midwife until she was able to open her own practice. It took the Riveras a few years to achieve a stable economic position that eventually allowed them to settle in a house one block from the Zocalo, the enormous city's central plaza.

Little Diego Rivera, in making his own adaptation to Mexico City, experienced some health problems and contracted scarlet fever and typhoid. He was sent to visit his great-aunt Vicenta. At her house he saw her collection of popular Mexican art, which undoubtedly influenced his later countless paintings and murals of popular Mexican motifs. At the time, however, the imaginative Diego had other ambitions that did not yet include art. He planned to become an engineer, to be the lover of a beautiful schoolgirl named Virginia Mena, and to be adored by the prostitutes who served the miners of Guanajuato.

As a young boy, Rivera was often characterized as mischievous and curious. He claimed to have had his first sexual experience with a teacher at the age of only nine. The story speaks about losing his virginity to his young American teacher at a Protestant school he was attending. Rivera's own account of his childhood was filled with interesting and shocking stories of his youth.

While living in Mexico City, Rivera enrolled in several schools, but did not last long in any of them on account of his devious behavior. One of the first schools he attended was the School of Father Antonio (Colegio del Padre Antonio), a clerical school chosen by his mother, but he had to leave after a few months because of his ill behavior. Rivera then was enrolled into Carpantier Catholic School, from which he would later also be expelled. But he was an intelligent child and entered another clerical school, Liceo Católico Hispano-Mexicano, as a third grader at the age of eight, only to be advanced up to sixth grade that same year. During his school time, Rivera did some sketches of fortifications and plans of battle that were highly praised by General Pedro Hinojosa, the minister of war of Mexico. Throughout his adolescence, Rivera would continue to draw and paint. Enabled by his natural artistic talent, Rivera applied to the Academy of San Carlos at the age of 10.

The Academy of San Carlos was a prestigious art school in Mexico that opened its doors in 1785. It was the first art school in all of Latin America and was run according to guidelines of the Spanish crown. The Academy of San Carlos followed European classical standards. This meant that the students had to draw details from reproductions of Rafaello and other similar High Renaissance artists. In addition, they worked many hours doing painting and sculpture copied from plaster cast models. An image that Rivera painted during this period in 1896 is titled *Classical Standing Figure Leaning on an Urn*. This drawing represents the influence of the classical ideas that the Academy of San Carlos was teaching at the time.

The Academy of San Carlos only enrolled men, and throughout the 18th and 19th centuries taught traditional art classes such as easel painting, sculpture, and drawing. In 1911, the students of the Academy of San Carlos went on strike against the director, Antonio Rivas Mercado, in protest of the rigidity and obsolescence of the teaching programs. The students were supported by a professor named Dr. Atl, who two years later became the new director of the Academy of San Carlos. Dr. Atl incorporated new standards for the academy that broke away from the European tradition. Artists began to create art that represented the political and national consciousness of Mexico.

Dr. Atl (Gerardo Murillo) was born in Guadalajara in 1875 and died in 1964. Dr. Atl began to paint at an early age and attended the Academy of San Carlos. While studying at the academy, he was sent to Europe to study art. When he returned to Mexico, he had revolutionary ideas that went against the traditional ways of teaching art. He began to gather together artists who had similar ideas and an attitude of rebellion against classical representations. It was while engaging in these projects that he met Diego Rivera.

Rivera was accepted into the Academy of San Carlos in December 1896 at the age of 10. He attended the academy during the night as well as attending elementary school during the day. He continued this schedule for two years and eventually received a scholarship that enabled him to attend the Academy of San Carlos during the day. While at the Academy of San Carlos, Rivera studied ideologies such as Comtean positivism, which insisted on eliminating supernatural explanations and only accepting objective reality. In other words, it was a philosophy that utilized the scientific method in the analysis of the natural world. At this time, Rivera was also exposed to ideas of naturalism, in which truth only exists in natural phenomena, and rationalism, the belief that all knowledge comes from reason.[6]

Some of the well-known teachers who instructed Rivera at the Academy of San Carlos were Félix Parra, José María Velasco, and Santiago Rebull. Félix Parra was a Mexican painter who had a passion for pre-Columbian art, which he communicated to the young Rivera, who would include this interest in the Mesoamerican cultures in the majority of his murals and eventually become an avid collector of Mesoamerican art.

José María Velasco was an extraordinary Mexican landscape painter whom Rivera admired and from whom he learned many techniques, such as the laws of perspective. It was through Velasco's teachings that Rivera was spared the stage of impressionism that he would have contacted at that date in Europe; Velasco's severely logical approach to optical problems prepared the young man instead for the further rationalizations of cubism. Rivera tells how the Mexican master introduced him to the classical concept of color when correcting one of his youthful works: "Boy, you cannot go on painting in that way. In the fore-ground you put side by side yellow spots for sunlight and blue spots for shadows; but yellow comes forwards and blue recedes, so that you destroy the very plane that you pretend to describe."[7] He described Velasco as "a completely scientific man, a student of geology, botany, natural history, meteorology, physics, and therefore mathematics." In reference to his teaching, Rivera said:

> The body of knowledge that Don José María Velasco made available to me was based on the geometry and trigonometry of space, and not on pure speculation but rather on the immediate apprehension of the plastic construction that transposed values of three or more dimensions on surfaces that are not only flat, but also concave, convex, and multifaceted. Everything that architectonic forms and surfaces have to offer in the way of represent-

able surfaces, and the transformation of volumes engendered upon those surfaces was always executed with a mathematical security.[8]

Rivera also began to paint outdoors, as Velasco had taught him. Painting outdoors was part of the positivist view of naturalism because it captured the world in its true reality. In 1904, Rivera painted *La Era* and *La Castañeda*, both examples of outdoor painting that also show perspective techniques he learned from Velasco. These two paintings earned Rivera the medal for teacher Antonio Fabrés's advanced painting class and were included in the annual December exhibition held by students in the Academy of San Carlos.

Santiago Rebull was another Mexican painter who instructed Rivera while at the Academy of San Carlos. Rebull, a man in his late 70s, was a pupil of Jean-Auguste Ingres and taught Rivera the laws of proportion, movement, and harmony. One day after a class he told Rivera that his drawing had some flaws, but he wanted to see him in his studio the next day because he was interested in what Rivera was doing. Rivera went to his studio and later wrote: "The old man told me that what he had discovered in my work was an interest in life and movement."[9]

Rebull was an important influence for Rivera's future cubist years and this is exemplified by a quote from Plato's *Socratic Dialogues*, which the old teacher recited to him. It was in reference to how, throughout the history of art, the great masters have always approached geometric forms and colors in their highest purity: "I wish to teach you to love, not beautiful fruits and women because flowers and fruit fade and women grow old. But rather, I wish to teach you to love the purest, permanent, and most imperishable forms, that it is to say, the figures that architects draw and construct: the cylinder, the cone, and the sphere; and the pure colors that correspond to them such as red, yellow, and blue; as we see them in a rainbow."[10] These instructors would greatly influence the techniques that would come to define Rivera's art throughout his career.

José Guadalupe Posada was not an instructor at the Academy of San Carlos, but would profoundly influence Rivera throughout his career as a painter. Posada was an engraver who owned a shop on Calle de la Moneda in Mexico City, which Rivera frequented. Posada began as an engraver often depicting satirical images of politicians as skeletons. Posada was not classically trained, but had a natural talent in depicting the culture and traditions of the Mexican people. Rivera stated: "It was he who revealed to me the inherent beauty in the Mexican people, their struggles and aspirations. And it was he who taught me the supreme lesson of all art—that nothing can be expressed except through the force of feeling, that the soul of every masterpiece is powerful emotion."[11] In the sketch titled *Merchant of Art,* Rivera is depicted looking over Posada's shoulder as he engraves. Rivera would continue to paint images inspired by Posada until his death in 1957.

During his time as a student at the Academy of San Carlos between 1898 and 1905, Rivera joined with other talented fellow classmates to form the *Grupo Bohemio.* Led by Dr. Atl, this group would come together to discuss poetry, art, music, and women while drinking beer and wine. *Grupo Bohemio* was not a politically motivated organization, but instead a group of students whose main interest was socializing about the art world.

In 1902, Rivera received a scholarship for the amount of 30 pesos a month from Teodoro A. Dehesa, who was the governor of the state of Veracruz. With this scholarship, Rivera was able to continue his studies. Aside from painting indoors, he began to paint in open air. In the painting titled *Landscape with Lake,* Rivera painted the scene using the outdoors as his model instead of a print. This technique revolutionalized landscape painting because an artist was able to paint nature in its most real form and space.

In 1904, continuing to use Dehesa's scholarship, Rivera enrolled in a course of human anatomy at the medical school in Mexico City. During his time at the medical school, Rivera began to study corpses in order to better understand human physiology. According to Rivera's own account, he learned about a French fur dealer who tried to improve the pelts of cats with a peculiar diet. The diet consisted of feeding cats with meat of other cats. The result was that the cats grew bigger, and their fur became firmer and finer. The French dealer surpassed his competitors, which gave Rivera an unusual idea. He convinced a group of fellow students to experiment in cannibalism with the purpose of seeing if this could improve their health. Rivera stated:

> Those of us who undertook the experiment pooled our money to purchase cadavers from the city morgue. We lived on this cannibal diet for two months, and everyone's health improved. During the time of our experiment, I discovered that I liked to eat the legs and breasts of women, for as in other animals, these parts are delicacies. I also savored young women's breaded ribs. Best of all however, I relished women's brains in vinaigrette.[12]

Even though it is possible to do an experiment of this kind, Rivera was infamous for creating stories. Rivera's habit of creating myths with the purpose of enhancing the uniqueness of his own persona and producing amazement in his audience often brought scandal from art critics and viewers. There is consensus among scholars that these cannibalistic claims never really happened.

Rivera continued to attend the Academy of San Carlos until he was expelled in 1905 for joining other students to organize and lead a demonstration that turned into a riot. The demonstration was organized against a priest accused of sexual corruption, but ultimately became a protest against the political system of the Mexican dictator Porfirio Díaz. Rivera protested, "Of all living men, Díaz was most to blame for the stultification of life and art in Mexico. And it is to him that Mexico, today, owes its wedding-cake palace architecture and insipid statuary."[13] Rivera was a liberal whose ideals went against the conservative government and whose goals were to transform Mexico into a modern society using Europe as a model.

During this time, Rivera joined *Savia Moderna*, a promodernist group of young artists, architects, writers, and intellectuals. The group published a magazine with the same name. In May 1906, Rivera and other artists participated in an exhibition organized by Dr. Atl for *Savia Moderna*. The exhibition incorporated artists who painted in modernistic styles influenced by impressionism, symbolism, and art nouveau.

Dr. Atl had returned from Europe in 1903 with European contemporary techniques and stories about art. As Dr. Atl began to teach in San Carlos, he became deeply impressed with the young Rivera. Inspired by Dr. Atl and his new ideas, Rivera began to make plans to go to Europe. In 1906, Rivera asked Governor Dehesa if he could fund his trip to Europe.

Teodoro Dehesa was a liberal and cultured man, and a lover of the arts. He believed in the transformation of humanity through education. He invested large amounts of money in new schools and he supported talented young men and women to achieve a higher education, so they could become teachers and leaders in his state of Veracruz. Dehesa agreed to give Rivera a scholarship under the condition that Rivera would create a one-man exhibition and sell his paintings in Mexico. If Rivera was successful, Governor Dehesa would fund his entire trip to Europe with a pension of 300 French francs to cover his living expenses for four years. With the help of Dr. Atl, Rivera put on a one-man show in the Academy of San Carlos and sold all his paintings displayed in the exhibition. With the money he made in the exhibition, he paid his ship passage to Europe and received the scholarship from Governor Dehesa.

A few months before leaving for Spain, Rivera went to paint in the countryside in the surroundings of the Orizaba Peak, the highest volcano in Mexico. In that region existed textile mills where workers worked long hours under inhumane conditions. The workers of the Rio Blanco textile factory resisted their exploitation and organized a strike. They sent a delegation to Mexico City to talk to President Díaz and look for a settlement of the situation. As the strike continued in Orizaba, Veracruz, the army repressed the workers with violence to make them to return to their work. The outcome was a massacre of dozens of men and women. Rivera witnessed dead bodies in the streets and in the plazas. He stopped painting and joined the strike. As a result he was beaten by a policeman and was imprisoned for several days. He later recalled that it was impelled by these scenes of such a brutal massacre that he boarded his ship for Spain and embarked upon a new European dream.

NOTES

1. Diego Rivera with Gladys March, *My Art, My Life: An Autobiography* (New York: Dover, 1991), 18.

2. Ibid., 2.

3. Patrick Marnham, *Dreaming with His Eyes Open: A Life of Diego Rivera* (New York: Knopf, 1998), 18–19.

4. Ibid.

5. Rivera, *My Art, My Life*, 6.

6. Laurence Hurlburt, *The Mexican Muralists in the United States* (Albuquerque: University of New Mexico Press, 1989), 27; Marnham, *Dreaming with His Eyes Open*.

7. Jean Charlot, "Diego Rivera at the Academy of San Carlos," *College Art Journal* 10, no. 1 (Autumn 1950): 10–17.

8. Ramón Favela, *Diego Rivera: The Cubist Years* (Phoenix, AZ: Phoenix Art Museum, 1984), 13.

9. Rivera, *My Art, My Life*, 17.

10. Diego Rivera, *Memoria y razón de Diego Rivera* (Mexico City: Renacimiento, 1959), 1:211–12; Favela, *Diego Rivera: The Cubist Years*, 16.

11. Rivera, *My Art, My Life*, 18.

12. Ibid., 20–21.

13. Ibid., 16; Bertram D. Wolfe, *The Fabulous Life of Diego Rivera* (New York: Stein & Day, 1963), 37.

Chapter 2

THE EUROPEAN PERIOD (1907–1921)

At the age of 20, Diego Rivera set off for Spain, arriving on January 6, 1907. With the help of Dr. Atl, Rivera was able to study with Eduardo Chicharro, one of the most famous realist artists in Spain at the time. Chicharro's work reflected mastery in the use of light and color, and he was the founder and first president of the Foundation for Painters and Sculptors. As Chicharro's disciple, Rivera painted from morning until night, dedicating most of his time to his art and the rest of the time to visiting Madrid's Prado Museum and other local galleries.

While in Spain, Rivera viewed the work of artists such as Hieronymus Bosch and Lucas Cranach, but Francisco Goya, Diego Velázquez, and El Greco were his preferred inspirations and he began to copy works by these three Spanish artists. Rivera later claimed that his copies were so precise that three of them can be found in well-known Goya collections in Paris and the United States. Rivera's claim only confirms his eccentric character, however, as none of these copies have ever been identified.

During his first year in Spain, Rivera befriended writers Ramón Gómez de la Serna and Ramón del Valle-Inclán, and painter Maria Gutiérrez Blanchard. Gómez de la Serna wrote more than 90 literary works, including *El Rastro* (The Flea-Market), *El Doctor Inverosímil* (The Improbable Doctor), *Greguerías* (Greguerias), and *Senos* (Breasts), which represent his nontraditional and modernistic method of writing. Del Valle-Inclán wrote *Divinas Palabras* (Divine Words) and *Luces Bohemias* (Bohemian Lights), which represent his criticism of the social norms practiced in Spain at this time. Gutiérrez Blanchard painted using color, line, and representation in a modern and liberated manner. These artists were influential avant-garde members of Spanish art circles and all had common ideas of change.

Some of the other writers who influenced Rivera during his time in Spain were Friedrich Nietzsche, Aldous Huxley, Emile Zola, Arthur Schopenhauer, Charles Darwin, (Francois-Marie Arouet) Voltaire, Peter Kropotkin, and Karl Marx. These writers not only influenced Rivera's artwork but also his beliefs throughout his life, with Marx as the most evident. In the mural titled *Man at the Crossroads* (1934), Rivera painted the demise of capitalism and included the images of Karl Marx and Vladimir Lenin. In most of Rivera's murals, he chose to include representations of his own beliefs, which were largely influenced by the writers he had read while in Europe.

After living in Spain for two years, Rivera decided to go to Paris, arriving there in the spring of 1909. While in Paris, Rivera stayed at the Hotel Suez, located in the Latin Quarter of Paris, where many artists from Spain and Latin America came to study. Interestingly enough, Rivera was given the same room that a fellow Mexican artist named Julio Ruelas had occupied earlier.

Ruelas, who had been Rivera's teacher in the Academy of San Carlos, was a symbolist painter who was active from 1892 to 1907 and was part of the early modern art movement in Mexico. Ruelas was one of the founders of the *Revista Moderna* (*Modern Magazine*), a modern art magazine later published under the name *Savia Moderna* (*Modern Vitality*). Rivera published several articles about his artwork in *Savia Moderna* between March and July 1906.

While in Paris, Rivera attended free lectures at the Academy of Montparnasse and in the evenings he socialized with other artists. It was in a Paris café that Rivera met a group of Russian exiles who further influenced his socialist views. Of this time period, Rivera later recalled, "In my paintings, I sought a way to incorporate my increasing knowledge and deepening emotions concerning social problems."[1] Although Rivera was becoming more familiar with and interested in socialist ideas, he did not begin to include socialist themes into his artwork until his return to Mexico.

In the summer of 1909, Rivera traveled to Bruges and Brussels in order to paint a different type of scenery. Rivera's first painting in Bruges was titled *House on the Bridge*. This painting differs from his prior work because he moved away from his linear composition and began to paint in an impressionistic manner. The lines drawn to represent images were now blurred, using color and shading to create a less rigid depiction of actual objects, in this case a house and bridge. This method softened Rivera's landscape work and enabled him to explore different lighting techniques.

In Bruges, Rivera met a young Russian painter named Angeline Beloff. Born in 1879 in St. Petersburg, Beloff's father, Michael Beloff, was a lawyer and her mother, Catherine Beloff, was a housewife. As a child, Angeline aspired to be a doctor but soon dropped out of medical school to enroll at the Academy of Fine Arts of Russia. She later moved to France where she attended art school and began to socialize with other art students, many of who were Russians. Rivera socialized in the same art circles, so it was almost inevitable that they would meet.

Rivera became enamored with Beloff but, since she spoke little Spanish and he spoke no French, he found it difficult to express his feelings. Beloff herself observed, "It seemed that Diego had made a declaration of love . . . directed at me, because he did not know how to tell me in French."[2] During this time, Rivera painted the image titled *Retrato de Angeline Beloff* (1909), executed in a traditional portraiture fashion, with a soft palette emphasizing her delicate qualities.

Before returning to Paris, Rivera traveled to London, where he took the opportunity to visit museums and study artwork by master painters such as J. M. William Turner and William Blake. Rivera was conscious of the influence of these romantic masters on modern art. He was eager to study their paintings but he also wanted to create sketches of London's industrial and slum areas.

Upon their return to France, Rivera and Beloff began to spend an increasing amount of time together. They would often go to cafés in the evening with fellow artist friends and spend the entire night drinking and discussing modern art, the routine for most artists in Paris at the time. The two eventually became lovers and were seen as a couple even though Rivera had other lovers.

Rivera continued to paint and study art in Paris. He would often go to art galleries to look at paintings by Paul Cézanne, Pablo Picasso, and other contemporary artists in Paris during this period. Rivera recalled the countless hours in which he would stand outside the window of the Ambroise Vollard gallery and stare in amazement at Cézanne's paintings, which were hanging in the window. He also visited the Louvre and studied Dutch artists, further enhancing his understanding of modern art.

In 1910, Rivera began to study with the impressionist painter Victor-Octave Guillonet. In 1915, Guillonet made a decisive change to producing art in a postimpressionist form. Before that time, however, Rivera painted *Breton Girl,* which illustrates Guillonet's impressionist influence. When we compare the more traditional *Portrait of Angeline* (1909) and the softer impressionistic *Breton Girl* (1910), one can see the drastic difference in technique, color, and use of light.

Although Rivera still mostly painted in the traditional classical style, he began to find interest in the new modernist movement in Paris. Rivera himself felt that, "My work of the period from 1909 through the first half of 1910, though it shows certain superiorities to my Spanish canvases, still looks academic and empty. But more potent, though I was little aware of it then, was my Mexican-American inferiority complex, my awe before historic European culture."[3] The cultural "inferiority complex" that Rivera felt he had during this period would eventually diminish as he matured as a painter in his native Mexico.

In 1910, as a result of his work while in Paris, Rivera was offered an exhibition in the Société des Artistes Indépendants. Rivera exhibited *House on the Bridge* and several other paintings such as *Head of a Breton Woman,* created during his trips to different parts of Europe. His long hours visiting and studying masters' techniques paid off in his first European exhibition.

In June 1910, Rivera went to Madrid to prepare for his exhibition in the Academy of San Carlos in Mexico. This exhibition was proposed by Governor Teodoro Dehesa, who had given Rivera the scholarship that enabled him to study in Europe. The exhibition was to coincide with the centennial celebration of Mexican independence.

In September 1910, Rivera sailed from Santander, Spain, to Mexico. Once Rivera arrived in Mexico, he stated that he was overcome with a feeling of connection to his life and culture. The Rivera that lacked self-confidence in Europe began to see the beauty and uniqueness of his homeland and the potential in himself. During Rivera's drive home after his arrival, he recounted the landscape and the feeling it gave him: "I was deeply moved by the panorama of landscape on my journey across the tropical and semitropical expanses of my homeland. When I finally reached the heights surrounding Mexico City, I could almost feel the landscape permeating me."[4]

Once Rivera reached his home on Jesús Maria Street in Mexico City, he was greeted by his parents, his sister, his *nana* (nanny) Antonia, and his dog Blackie. The immense welcome overwhelmed him so much that he fainted. He described waking up several days later to find out that he had been in a coma. Rivera was bedridden for some time with a high fever, and his childhood *nana*, Antonia, stayed by his side. According to Rivera, a doctor came to see him and left him some medication, but Antonia would not let him take it. Instead, Antonia, an indigenous woman who believed in homeopathic and herbal medicine, took it upon herself to cure Rivera, who had been like her son since his youth in the forests of Michoacán.

Antonia began her preparation with a ritual involving an egg, which symbolized the transference of the spirit of life from one thing to another. She gave the egg to Rivera after she had placed it between her breasts and pierced it at both ends with a needle. She then kissed the egg and asked Rivera to do the same and drink it. After this ritual, Antonia began to chant in her native tongue, Tarascan, and threw the shell, the needle, and a small bag in the fire she had built in the kitchen. She began to fan the fire while still chanting, kissed Rivera, and asked him to continue fanning the flames until all that was left were ashes, and then exited the house. The next day the Rivera family looked for Antonia, but she never returned.

Rivera fully recovered and began to prepare for his upcoming exhibition, all while Mexico was under political turmoil. When Rivera arrived in Mexico in October 1910, Francisco I. Madero was running for president against Porfirio Díaz, who had been in office since 1876, 10 years before Rivera's birth. Before the election, Madero was exiled to the United States by Díaz's party, forcing Madero out of the candidacy and securing the presidency for Díaz. In response, Madero initiated the Mexican Revolution with the *Plan of San Luis Potosi*, a statement calling for all Mexican citizens to stand in arms on November 20, 1910, against Díaz and his party. Interestingly enough, that same day Díaz's wife, Carmen Romero Rubio de Díaz, officially inaugurated Diego Rivera's exhibition at the Academy of San Carlos. The exhibition was very successful, with Rivera selling 13 of his 40 paintings to Díaz's wife and the government of Mexico.

In 1911, while Rivera was still in Mexico, the revolutionaries Francisco (Pancho) Villa and Emiliano Zapata began to fight in the north and south of Mexico against the Mexican government's monopoly over land and power. Although the revolution began with noble ideals, the result was 10 years of suffering by the Mexican people. Food and other essentials became scarce. Many people lost their homes to looting and many innocent people were killed. There were many rebels who fought not against the government, but rather used the war to steal land and food for themselves and to rape children and women. In 1911 the revolutionaries took control of Juarez City on the border of Mexico and Texas. This made it difficult for Díaz to escape Mexico from the north and forced him to find a way out through the south. Eventually, he went into exile in Paris, France.

Rivera ideologically allied himself with the revolutionary movement and during his short stay in Mexico, he claimed that he and a group of friends had created a plot to kill President Díaz, an action that scholars think is fictional.

During his last few months in Mexico, Rivera arranged for another exhibition in order to sell his paintings so that he could return to Europe. Rivera was assisted by his friends Francisco Urquidi, Secretary of the School of Fine Arts, Lino Lebrija who was the director of the school, and José María Velasco and Felix Parra, two of his former teachers. Rivera, in his autobiography, also mentions José Guadalupe Posada as his teacher and participant in the assassination plot, but in a strict sense Posada never was his teacher nor participated in such an incident. Knowing that President Díaz was going to attend the exhibition, Rivera, Lebrija, and Eduardo Hay, an architect, conspired to assassinate President Díaz on the opening day of the exhibition. Rivera's role was to smuggle explosives into the school where the exhibition was to be held. A short time after Rivera gave the explosives to Lebrija, who put them into the school safe, the police arrived to inspect the school. The police did not search the safe; nevertheless the plan could not be completed because President Díaz did not attend the exhibition. Instead, Carmen Romero Rubio de Díaz, the president's wife, arrived as the president's representative. The plan to assassinate President Díaz was a failure, but the exhibition was a success.

With the sales that Rivera made from his art show, he now had enough money to return to Europe to continue his studies and reunite with Beloff. Instead, Rivera traveled south to join Zapata's rebels in the state of Morelos. After six months, Rivera took a train to Jalapa, Mexico, to meet with Governor Dehesa. Upon arriving in Jalapa, a group of rebels entered the train to ask for donations for the revolutionary cause. Rivera gave some money to the revolutionaries and continued on his path to see the governor who, although he was part of Díaz's government, was seen as a liberal and therefore was protected by the rebels. Rivera stayed with Governor Dehesa for a couple of weeks before leaving for Europe in June 1911.

When Rivera reached Paris late in June, he resumed his relationship with Beloff and they moved into 26 de Rue de Depart, where they lived together for the next 10 years. Rivera also started a friendship with painter Amedeo Modigliani, an Italian artist who lived most of his career in France. Rivera and Modigliani were often seen in cafés drinking and taking part in mischievous behaviors, such as telling dirty words to the pedestrians. It was during this time that Rivera painted *Catalonian Landscape* (1911). This landscape scene represents a definitive move toward a different technique that Rivera had not used before. He began to be influenced by neoimpressionist and divisionist methods, which can be seen in the *Catalonian Landscape* through the pointillism technique.

In the spring of 1912, Rivera and Beloff traveled to Toledo, Spain, to visit the museums and galleries. While in Toledo, Rivera painted *View of Toledo* (1912) and *Landscape of Toledo* (1913), landscape scenes that show he was beginning to develop his cubist style. When he returned to Paris in the fall, Rivera reunited with Angel Zárraga, Dr. Atl, Roberto Montenegro, and Adolfo Best Maugard, Mexican artists who were living in Paris during the time Rivera lived there and who experimented with cubism as well. The friendship with Zárraga and other artists, such as Piet Mondrian, Conrad Kikkert, and Lodewijk Schelfhout, is precisely what influenced Rivera to paint in the cubist style.

By 1912–1913, Rivera had reached his cubist stage and later explained, "It was the revolutionary movement, questioning everything that had previously been said and done in art. It held nothing sacred. As the old world would soon blow itself apart, never to be the same again, so cubism broke down forms as they had been seen for centuries, and was creating out of the fragments, new forms, new objects, new patterns and—ultimately—new worlds. When it dawned on me that all this innovation had little to do with real life, I would surrender all the glory and acclaim cubism had brought me for a way in art truer to my inmost feelings."[5] During Rivera's cubist period, he created more than 200 paintings and exhibited at several galleries such as the Salon d'Automne. One of the paintings that Rivera exhibited in 1912 in the Salon d'Automne was the Zuloagesque *Portrait of a Spaniard* that shows a realist and powerful rendition of the personage.

After the exhibition ended, Rivera returned to Toledo to prepare six paintings for his approaching *Groupe Libre* exhibition at the Galerie Bernheim-Jeune, which opened in January 1913. Once the *Groupe Libre* exhibition was finished, he immediately began to work for his spring exhibition in the Société des Artistes Indépendants. It was in this group exhibition that Rivera showed several cubist paintings including *Retrato de Adolfo Best Maugard*. This painting was especially important to Rivera's career because it finally marked his acceptance into the art world in Paris.

That same year in 1913, Rivera lost his financial aid from the Mexican government consequent to the assassination of President Madero and Vice President Pino Suárez, which marked the continuation of the Mexican civil war that would last another seven years. The loss of government financing forced Rivera to sell all his paintings in order to support himself and Beloff. With the help of his friends Robert Delaunay, Fernand Léger, and Marc Chagall, he sold every painting. The majority of these paintings were presented in temporary exhibitions in Munich and Vienna.

In the summer of 1913, Rivera returned to Paris and painted *Girl with Artichokes* and *Woman with a Fan*. He submitted these two paintings into an exhibition at the Salon D'Automne in order to show his diverse representations of the human figure. Rivera received wide acclaim for *Woman with a Fan* and was asked for permission to reproduce the image in several journals.

Rivera also began to paint images combining cubism and futurism. "Futurism was an artistic movement with political implications which sought to free Italy from the oppressive weight of her past, and glorified the modern world—machinery, speed, violence—in a series of exuberant manifestos."[6] In the image titled *Woman at the Well* (1913), Rivera incorporated geometrical forms and activated them by creating movement with the use of space, thus successfully combining these two modern movements within one painting.

In 1914, Rivera painted *Sailor at Lunch* and *Two Women*, which incorporated a compositional grid (a grid that an artist creates on a canvas in order to follow the image more closely). The artist then paints over the grid using it as a guide. Rivera used a compositional grid to help him create a cubist image in a more exact manner. The two paintings in which Rivera used the compositional grid were both submitted into the Sociéte des Artistes Indépendants exhibition. He learned many techniques such as compositional grid and mixing of material like sand into pigment from the Spanish cubist artist Juan Gris.

Rivera knew he had reached fame among the avant-garde movement in Paris when he was introduced in early 1914 to Pablo Picasso by Chilean artist Manuel Ortíz de Zárate. Ortíz de Zárate took Rivera to meet Picasso at his studio, where they discussed art and viewed the paintings that Picasso was working on at the time. After this meeting, they became good friends and would go to cafés and galleries in Paris together. Sometime later, Rivera and Picasso had a falling-out, which primarily had to do with the image titled *The Paisaje Zapatista—La Guerrilla* that Picasso painted in 1915. Rivera accused Picasso of plagiarizing techniques he used to represent negative space. Rivera later said, "It seems to me that, in every one of his periods, Picasso has shown more imagination than originality, that everything he has done is based upon the work of somebody else."[7] Although Rivera had initially admired Picasso for his "mastery of cubism," he became offended by Picasso's act of disparagement.[8]

After Rivera publicly vocalized his disapproval of Picasso's actions, most of the art community in Paris, including critics, began to snub Rivera and his art. In 1917, Pierre Reverdy, an art critic and poet, published an essay defining cubism and attacking cubist painters. After a dinner held for painters by Léonce Rosenberg, Rivera and Reverdy got into a quarrel at André Lhote's apartment. In a letter sent from Max Jacob to a friend, Jacob comments about this argument: "While we became livelier and livelier in the studio, Pierre arrogantly raised himself up on the Cubist pedestal: he treated his friends there with such little respect that Monsieur Rivera felt insulted and slapped him without regard for his oratory talent. The young and ardent theoretician of Cubism, in whose heart runs courageous blood, leaped upon his insulter and they both forgot about the present, those present, and precedence. Reverdy yanked Rivera's hair while screaming: the crowd of people there threw themselves on the combatants. The unfortunate Madame Lhote had tears in her eyes."[9] After the ordeal was over, Rivera offered an apology that Reverdy did not accept. The painters, dealers, and critics took sides and Rivera was ostracized by the Paris art community. Rosenberg withdrew some of Rivera's paintings from the art market including the *Zapatista Landscape* painting. This ordeal became known as *l'affaire Rivera*.

In April, Rivera was given his first solo exhibition in the gallery of Berthe Weill located in Paris. He submitted 25 works including *Young Man with Stylograph* (1913–1914). All of Rivera's works that were submitted were painted in the cubist style. In the catalogue made for Rivera's exhibition, Weill wrote a negative comment about cubism in the foreword and caused some discomfort, but the exhibition was still a financial success.

In the summer of 1914, Rivera, Beloff, Jacques Lipchitz, Berthe Kristover, and Maria Gutiérrez Blanchard traveled to Spain to sketch their surroundings. While they were in the Spanish island of Majorca, World War I began. The artists, including Rivera, used this opportunity to paint the lush environment that the island had to offer. Once the group of artists was able to leave the island, they traveled to Madrid, where they joined avant-garde artists like the Dadaists. The Dada movement was an anarchic revolt against traditional values. They again encountered the avant-garde writer Ramón Gómez de la Serna, who had become a Dada poet. There in Madrid, Gómez de la Serna organized an exhibition titled *Los Pintores Integros* (The Integral Painters), which included Rivera. The objective of the exhibition was to introduce cubism to Madrid. The exhibit produced a scandalous reaction of the audience because the nature of cubism attacked the forms of traditional painting, and the authorities shut down the gallery. A few months later, Rivera exhibited his cubist work in New York for the Society of Independent Artists' first annual exhibition.

On August 11, 1916, Angeline Beloff gave birth to a child they named Diego Rivera Jr. The cold winter weather, the lack of money, and World War I all became hardships that the child could not survive. Bertram D. Wolfe, Rivera's friend and later biographer, remembered that, "Fuel was unobtainable, milk, also, often food of any sort. Water froze in the pipes, the municipal pumping system broke down for the lack of coal to run the engines. Diego and Angeline were able to stand it, but for the little boy it was too much; he died before the year was out, one of the innumerable, uncounted victims of the war."[10] The little Diego was buried in a common grave in the historical cemetery of Pére Lachaise. This misfortune would not be the last for Beloff, as later that year Rivera left her to live with another lover named Marievna Vorobiev-Stebelska.

Vorobiev was a Russian artist who met Rivera through the notable writer Ilya Ehrenburg. Ehrenburg later wrote a novel based on Rivera's childhood titled *Julio Jurenito* (1921). Not long after Rivera and Vorobiev met, they became lovers and Rivera left Beloff for Vorobiev. Rivera lived with Vorobiev for half a year until the relationship failed. Soon after, Rivera returned to Beloff and resumed his relationship with her. Several months passed and Rivera received several visits from Vorobiev, who was visibly pregnant. Rivera stated that when the child was born, Vorobiev brought her around to show as proof of their relationship. Once the child Marika was grown, she wrote many letters to Diego, but he never responded. Diego stated that he never felt the need to revisit the past and that both Marievna and Marika never needed him.

Between 1916 and 1918, Diego Rivera painted very little. In 1917, he met physician and art historian Élie Faure, who sponsored a group exhibition titled *Les Constructeurs* (The Constructors), which included Rivera. Faure encouraged Rivera to stop painting in the cubist style and explore other styles and forms, like Italian art. Rivera returned to realism, leaving cubism behind. The painting titled *El Matemático* (*The Mathematician*) is an example of his return to realism. Alberto J. Pani, the Mexican ambassador in France, purchased *The Mathematician*. Pani recommended that Rivera return to Mexico to paint for Carranza's government, but Rivera felt that he was not ready.

In 1919, David Alfaro Siqueiros traveled to Paris as a military attaché in the Mexican embassy. There he met Rivera for the first time. While there, both artists discussed the events of the Mexican Revolution and the social and political implications it had for Mexican art. With the assassination of Zapata by President Carranza, Mexico was undergoing many changes that led General Alvaro Obregón to become a candidate for the presidency. As President Carranza did not support Obregón's candidacy, in 1920 by orders of Obregón, Carranza was murdered.

Under Obregón's presidency, the philosopher and writer José Vasconcelos was appointed as the secretary of public education in Mexico in 1921. Realizing that 90 percent of the population of Mexico was illiterate, Vasconcelos began a new educational program that included a literacy campaign through the painting of murals in public buildings. The muralist movement would serve to educate the illiterate masses, as painted books on the walls, teaching the history and political events of Mexico.

Vasconcelos wanted to include Rivera in the mural program and petitioned him to travel to Italy to study the Renaissance mural works. The idea was that Rivera could gain more valuable knowledge and training through direct study of the frescos of the great masters. When the offer came from Vasconcelos to travel to Italy, Faure encouraged Rivera to take the opportunity. Faure would prove to be a long-lasting friend and mentor to Rivera until his death.

In 1920, Rivera traveled to Italy to study the mural art of the late Gothic and Renaissance periods. He visited Ravenna, Florence, Siena, Arezzo, Perugia, Assisi, Rome, Naples, Messina, Padua, and Venice.

In those cities, he studied the works of Giotto, Uccello, Masaccio, Mantegna, Tintoretto, Piero della Francesca, Michelangelo, Raphael, Gozzoli, and Antonello da Messina. Rivera actually spent six months studying the fresco paintings, although he later claimed in his autobiography that he stayed in Italy for 17 months before he returned to Paris. In that time, Rivera gained immense knowledge about muralism and returned with more than 300 sketches from frescoes of the master Italian Renaissance painters.

Before Rivera could return to Mexico, however, he had to sell his paintings in order to raise money for the trip. In October 1920, Rivera participated in an *Exposicion d'art Francais d'avant-garde* at the Galerie Dalman in Barcelona. He also participated in another exhibition in New York in December, which was titled *Sociéte Anonyme*. Some artists who were included in the New York exhibition were Matisse, Picasso, Jacques Villon, Georges Braque, André Derain, Albert Gleizes, and Juan Gris. Rivera sold the paintings he had in Paris at the time and left behind Angeline Beloff, Marievna Vorobiev-Stebelska, and his daughter Marika.

In a letter later written to Rivera by his friend in Paris, Élie Faure wrote, "You ought to write from time to time to poor Angelina, whom I see sometimes, not as often as when you were here. . . . She leads ever her valiant and solitary life, awaiting your return or a call from you."[11] Rivera left Paris without a definitive conclusion to his relationship with Beloff, and she continued to wait for him for some time. Beloff sent many letters to Rivera over the years, stating her dedication to the love which they had shared.

> It is very difficult for me, Diego, to write you. Here it is a year since you left. I have not forgotten you, I have even forgotten you too little for the lapse of time. . . .
>
> What hurts is to think that you no longer have any need of me at all—none at all. . . . Painful, yes, but indispensable to know. . . . You have had plenty of time to reflect and make up your mind at least unconsciously, if you have not had any occasion to formulate it. Well then, formulate it. . . . Otherwise we will come to useless suffering, useless and monotonous like a toothache, and with the same result. You see, you do not write me—you will write less and

> less if we let time run on; in a few years we will meet as strangers if we meet at all. As for me, I can say that the toothache will continue down till the root rots away to the bottom—well then, is it not better to pull out the tooth if you find nothing in you that draws you to me?[12]

Many letters were written to Rivera upon his arrival to Mexico and many would continue for some time after. The obvious anguish displayed in the letters show her commitment to their relationship. Rivera responded to Beloff by bidding her to come to Mexico, but without responding to her plea for a clear answer about their relationship and without sending any money for her trip. Years later, in 1932, Beloff traveled to Mexico and lived the remainder of her life there, although she only saw Rivera once, to sign some drawings she had from when they lived in Paris together.

NOTES

1. Diego Rivera with Gladys March, *My Art, My Life: An Autobiography* (New York: Dover, 1991), 30.
2. Pete Hamill, *Diego Rivera* (New York: Abrams, 2002), 36.
3. Rivera, *My Art, My Life*, 30–31.
4. Ibid., 42.
5. Ibid., 58.
6. Ian Chilvers and Harold Osborne, *The Oxford Dictionary of Art* (New York: Oxford University Press, 1988), 211.
7. Hamill, *Diego Rivera*, 68.
8. Ibid., 69.
9. Quoted in Ramon Favela, *Diego Rivera: The Cubist Years* (Phoenix, AZ: Phoenix Art Museum, 1984), 110.
10. Bertram Wolf, *The Fabulous Life of Diego Rivera* (New York: Cooper Square Press, 1963), 101.
11. Ibid., 123.
12. Ibid., 125–26.

Chapter 3

MURALS OF THE 1920s

In the years prior to the arrival of Rivera to Mexico in 1921, Mexico was undergoing great political turmoil. The same year that Diego left for Europe for the second time, President Díaz went into exile in Paris and Francisco I. Madero became president. In defiance, revolutionaries Emiliano Zapata and Otilio Montaño created *The Plan de Ayala,* which demanded the distribution of land among the less privileged citizens of Mexico. In 1913, Madero and his vice-president Pino Suárez were assassinated by orders of Minister of Defense General Victoriano Huerta. With the political and economic support of the United States through ambassador Henry Lane Wilson, Huerta was put in charge of the Mexican government, while the revolution continued for another seven years. Agriculture, industrial production, transportation, and communications were left in ruins by the bandits, who controlled a large part of the country. In 1917, Venustiano Carranza officially became president of Mexico and created its current constitution, but he was assassinated in 1920. That same year, Álvaro Obregón was elected president.

When Rivera arrived in Mexico one year later, he was reborn in his art and his life. He immediately began to paint all of the colorful surroundings that made up his native country. He no longer felt inferior as a Mexican artist, as he had in Europe. For several months, Rivera worked as an easel painter, advisor for a publishing house, chief of propaganda for the government, and director of a workers' school, activities that were all unsatisfying for his artistic ambitions. Finally, in October 1921, Minister of Education José Vasconcelos, with the recommendation of Dr. Atl, commissioned Rivera to paint a mural at the National Preparatory School of the University of Mexico.

Dr. Atl (Gerardo Murillo) was a painter who studied and taught at the Academy of San Carlos in Mexico City. Although Dr. Atl was radical and nationalistic in his political views, he had traveled to Europe between 1896 and 1903 to further his comprehension of the great fresco masters such as Michelangelo, Leonardo da Vinci, and Rafael, and to study law and philosophy at the University of Rome. Back in Mexico in 1910, he created a group called Centro Artístico (Artistic Center). The Centro Artístico was established to create a nationalistic art with the objective of painting decorative murals on the walls of public buildings following the aesthetic principles of *modernism.* In Latin America, *modernismo* developed as a literary and artistic movement between 1880 and 1910, and consisted of rejecting the quotidian experience and examining the quest for beauty and the perfection of forms.

Young and enthusiastic artists participated in the modernist movement in Mexico, such as Clemente Orozco, who helped Dr. Atl in his purpose of developing an art that would express a spontaneous energy, spiritualism, and symbolism. Dr. Atl also obtained permission from Justo Sierra, minister of education under Díaz, to paint a mural with scenes of female nudes in the National Preparatory School in Mexico City. Upon the advent of the Mexican Revolution, however, the project was suspended and the walls of the Preparatory School remained untouched. In 1913, Dr. Atl returned a second time to Europe where he continued to refine his mural techniques. Upon his return to Mexico, he became a controversial and revolutionary director of the Academy of San Carlos. Dr. Atl opposed the pure academicism of the time and envisioned the joining of the art institution to the social and political revolution as a necessary action. He has been credited as the ideological father of Mexican muralism and of the modern school of painting in Mexico in light of his influence on the young painters of the period.

The common thread between Dr. Atl and Minister of Education Vasconcelos was their interest in philosophy and revolutionary ideological beliefs. Vasconcelos was an attorney but had found himself exiled to Paris as punishment for his opposition to President Huerta. While in Paris, Vasconcelos and Dr. Atl met and exchanged ideas. Upon Vasconcelos and Dr. Atl's return to Mexico, they were fundamental to setting in motion the birth of Mexican muralism.

As the minister of public education in Mexico from 1921 to 1924, Vasconcelos facilitated the intellectual and artistic vision promoted and implemented by artists such as Dr. Atl. Vasconcelos allowed a plethora of books and magazines to be published, but there was still the task of educating an overwhelmingly illiterate Mexican population. He supported Dr. Atl's idea of using murals to communicate artistic and sociopolitical values to the public with the purpose of educating the citizenry. Vasconcelos offered artists commissions from the government to paint public walls. He then allowed artists the liberty to paint what they felt was necessary in order to produce what had been defined by one scholar as "an art saturated with primitive vigor, new subject matter, combining subtlety and the sacrifice of the exquisite to the great, perfection to invention."[1] It was one of the paradoxes of his time that an idealist philosopher such as Vasconcelos would help launch a movement in which the artists would eventually reject his idealism in favor of a partisan and often didactic art.

In 1921, Vasconcelos commissioned the first murals at the chapel of El Colegio de San Pedro y San Pablo, a former Jesuit School in Mexico City. Among the participant artists there were Dr. Atl, Roberto Montenegro, Xavier Guerrero, Gabriel Fernández Ledesma, and Jorge Enciso. Immediately after came the murals at the National Preparatory School, where the commissioned artists were Diego Rivera, David Alfaro Siqueiros, Clemente Orozco, Jean Charlot, Fermín Revueltas, Xavier Guerrero, Amado de la Cueva, and Ramón Alva de la Canal.

The National Preparatory School was built in 1588 and was originally the Jesuit School called Colegio de San Ildefonso. It later merged with the Colegio de San Pedro y San Pablo. With the Laws of Reform implemented by President Juárez in Mexico in 1867, San Ildefonso was secularized and renamed the National Preparatory School. During the time Francisco Madero was in office from 1911 to 1913, José

Vasconcelos was the director of the National Preparatory School. He changed the curriculum and broke with the positivistic influences left by the *Porfiriato*. Later, as minister of education, he returned to the National Preparatory School to implement his first educational project.

Vasconcelos commissioned Rivera to paint in the Bolívar Amphitheatre in the National Preparatory School. Before the mural was begun, Vasconcelos invited Rivera and a group of artists to travel to Yucatán, where they visited archaeological sites such as Chichén Itzá and Uxmal to familiarize themselves with their Mexican heritage and culture. Vasconcelos wanted the artists to create murals that would represent Mexico.

In 1922, Rivera began to paint his first mural, titled *Creation*. He was assisted by Carlos Mérida, Jean Charlot, Amado de la Cueva, and Xavier Guerrero. The first obstacle for Rivera was to integrate his painting into the structural forms of the Baroque Colonial style amphitheater. He was given the back wall of the center stage, which measures almost 1,000 square feet. The ceiling wall is arched with two pillars on either side. In the middle of the wall there is a small concave space that holds the pipe organ. Rivera integrated the dimensions and proportions of the wall space with the composition, which resulted in a monumental allegorical scene.

The structural aspect of the mural proved not the only obstacle for Rivera. Another challenge was in selecting the material and technique he would use on the wall. While in Italy, he had learned the techniques of the great fresco painters and decided to use this similar medium. He attempted to utilize an old book on the techniques of Italian fresco painting written by Cellino Cennini, but the problem was that many of the ingredients used did not exist or were not known in Mexico. Thus, his first mural was executed in the difficult medium of *encaustic*. Encaustic is a method of wax painting that dates to antiquity in Greece and Italy. The process consists of heating beeswax and mixing pigments into the liquid paste. The wax is then applied to the surface of the wall or panel.

> This procedure, which Rivera restored by his own efforts, thanks to research made during some ten years, is the most solid of the painting processes (in inalterability, resistance, and duration) except for fired enamel.[2]

Rivera eventually abandoned the wax *encaustic* method and started to use a more practical fresco technique similar to the one used by the ancient Teotihuacán people, as he and one of his assistants Xavier Guerrero noticed in their trips to the ancient city. The nationalistic atmosphere of the time helped to legitimize the use of fresco based on its connections with the pre-Columbian historical past.

The next decision Rivera had to make was the choice of theme and subject matter. He began to paint a "poetic and philosophical medley of Christianity and paganism; symbols of knowledge and wisdom, constellations, halos and angels' wings alternate in it with muses and the three cardinal virtues."[3] Rivera neglected to paint national themes as Vasconcelos had hoped and as would come to define Mexican muralism. Just before the mural was complete, at the end of 1922, Vasconcelos sent Rivera on another trip, this time to Tehuantepec to further immerse him in the country's heritage and traditions. In Tehuantepec, Rivera began to understand what Vasconcelos wanted of him. He was immersed in the unique characteristics that would come to represent Mexican muralism: the lush forests, the indigenous people, and the bright array of colors found in the *mercados* (outdoor markets). Once he returned to Mexico City, he began to incorporate more Mexican themes and colors into his "poetic and philosophical composition." Although much of the *Creation* mural was finished by the time he went to Tehuantepec, he returned to integrate animals that symbolized Mexican mythological stories and women who had indigenous qualities.

Some of the depictions included after Rivera's trip to Tehuantepec are the depiction of the indigenous female who represents wisdom as well as the center panel where the Mexican fertile landscape is represented with its indigenous animals. The trip helped Rivera realize his potential and more clearly identify himself as a Mexican painter. In his journal, Rivera gave an explanation of how the *Creation* mural represented various forms of creation through humanity, reason, and nature. In the mural, he depicted man emerging from a tree of life flanked by allegorical figures that represent the emanations of the spirits of man and woman.

In 1922, while Rivera was painting the mural at the National Preparatory School, he met Guadalupe Marín, an actress of great beauty and strong personality. He was immediately captivated by Marín and the two soon became inseparable. He described her as a beautiful, tall woman with translucent green eyes and indigenous facial features with strong legs, which attracted him.

Soon after meeting, Rivera and Marín married in Guadalajara and moved close to the Zocalo (Central Plaza) in Mexico City. Rivera used Marín as a model for the *Creation* mural, in which she is depicted as the seated nude woman (Eve) to the left of the tree, and as an embodiment of Song and Justice.

While Rivera was painting the *Creation* mural, he and fellow painters David Alfaro Siqueiros, Carlos Mérida, Amado de la Cueva, Ramón Alva Guadarrama, Xavier Guerrero, Fernando Leal, Fermín Revueltas, and Hernán Queto formed the Sindicato Revolucionario de Obreros Técnicos y Plásticos (Revolutionary Union of Technical Workers, Painters, Sculptors, and Allied Trades). The union was created as a community of artists with a common goal of perpetuating socialistic ideas through art and muralism. The group's credo read:

> *Revolutionary*—they would transform the world, and art was to aid in the transformation.
>
> *Union*—to defend the interest of their craft, to win a place for social painting, conquer walls, reconquer the right to speak to the people.
>
> *Workers*—down with aestheticism, ivory towers, long-haired exquisites! Art was to don overalls, climb the scaffold, engage in collective action, reassert its craftsmanship, take sides in the class struggle.
>
> *Painters, Sculptors, and Allied Trades*—did they not all work with their hands? Were they not building-trades workers—like plasterers, stone-cutters, glaziers, cement-pourers? They would unite with the rest of the producers, clarify by their paintings the consciousness of the most important class in modern society, be supported and defended by it, join it in the building of a workers' world.[4]

The union wanted to form a kinship with people who were not yet legitimized as artists. Potters, basket weavers, wood carvers, and textile weavers were looked at as peasant workers and not true artists. The union called all artists and craftsmen who worked with their hands to join them in the struggle to educate the masses. They also understood the importance of murals in Mexico. Muralism became a didactic tool to express the social and political climate in Mexico after the Mexican Revolution.

The union also printed pamphlets of information about the views of the organization. The pamphlets eventually became known as the newspaper *El Machete* and ultimately the journal of the Mexican Communist Party. *El Machete* was sold for 10 cents, a low enough price to enable the working class to obtain it. *El Machete*'s motto was "The machete serves to cut the cane, to open paths in shadowed woods, to decapitate serpents, to cut down weeds, and to humble the pride of the impious rich."[5] The editors for the newspaper/journal were Xavier Guerrero, David Alfaro Siqueiros, and Diego Rivera. *El Machete*'s primary goal was to assert rights in the unionization of artists, including craftsmen and other artists alike. The journal was a place where artists could express their political and social beliefs and show how art had a role to perpetuate social change. *El Machete* reflected the idea that art had to represent real historical context in order to foster political goals.

In December 1922, Rivera joined the Communist Party. Rivera quickly moved up the ranks in 1923 and became a member of the Communist Party's Executive Committee. *El Machete* was used as the source of disseminating communist ideology. In 1923, Rivera accepted a commission to work on the patio of the Secretaría de Educación Pública (Ministry of Public Education), which did not allow him to dedicate any time to *El Machete*.

From 1922 to the end of 1923, Mexican artists began to move toward depicting nationalistic themes and Mexico was becoming widely known for mural painting. Artists in Paris, Latin America, and the United States began to see Mexico's new muralist movement as the most important since the Renaissance.[6] Vasconcelos invited artists like David Alfaro Siqueiros, José Clemente Orozco, and Fermín Revueltas, along with Diego Rivera, to continue painting under the payroll of the education department.

Soon after the inauguration of the *Creation* mural in 1923, Vasconcelos appointed Rivera as head of the Department of Plastic Crafts at the newly created Ministry of Education, opened in 1921 by President Obregón. The construction of the ministry's new building became a symbol to exemplify the radical education policies of Vasconcelos. Rivera was asked to create a mural that reflected Vasconcelos's goal. In 1924, Vasconcelos became displeased with President Obregón's policies and resigned from the Ministry of Education. With Vasconcelos's resignation, Siqueiros and Orozco were dismissed, but Rivera successfully continued with his project at the Ministry of Education under the new minister of education, José Manuel Puig Cassauranc, who was an intelligent and cultured man.

The colossal cycle of murals at the Ministry of Education became one of the most spectacular achievements of Rivera's career. It took Rivera four years and three months, working 18-hour days, to complete this mural consisting of 235 panels (128 principal works) done in fresco and measuring 1,600 square meters, or about 17,000 square feet. The two patios are each surrounded by three floors containing painted panels.

After Rivera's *Creation* mural was made in *encaustic*, he began to incorporate the fresco method into his murals. The fresco method consists of applying pigment onto a wall that has been covered with wet plaster. Once the plaster dries, the pigment and plaster fuse together to create a durable mural that will resist the environmental elements. The fresco technique proved to be a very reliable and much easier method than *encaustic*, and therefore most muralists chose to use it.

Rivera's second mural project in the Ministry of Education was drastically different from the first. Rivera had received much criticism because the *Creation* mural did not represent themes that were indicative of the muralist movement. His first mural became the antithesis of what Mexican muralism was becoming. In the Ministry of Education, Rivera embarked on a new representation that would characterize his work and the movement for the rest of his career.

The thematic scheme for the Ministry of Education building expresses the social and political reality in Mexico during and after the revolution. The nationalistic iconography depicted in its various panels shows indigenous people, landscapes, and social struggles. The huge building is composed of two large patios. Rivera titled the first patio the *Courtyard of Labor,* a cycle that includes 18 panels. Located on the first floor, the cycle depicts activities of the Mexican people, mainly related to industrial and agricultural production.

On the north wall of the first level of the *Courtyard of Labor* in the Ministry of Education, Rivera painted *The Weavers*, *The Dyers*, and *The Tehuanas*. On the first level of the east wall he painted a Náhuatl poem with images to go along with the poem. The titles are *Entering the Mine*, *Leaving the Mine*, *Embrace*, *Peasants*, *Foreman*, and *Pottery Markers*. The south wall includes the *Foundry: Opening the Smelter*, *Surface Miners*, *Liberation of the Peon*, *Rural Schoolteacher*, *Shepherd with Sling*, and *Foundry—Pouring the Crucible*. In this cycle, Rivera included raw products that are indigenous to Mexico, such as textiles, corn, and mining. Although Rivera was an atheist, he used biblical and religious symbols to parallel the lives of the indigenous people of Mexico. This was a didactic strategy in order to communicate more effectively with the Mexican Catholic population.

On the north wall of the second level of the *Courtyard of Labor* in the Ministry of Education there are seven murals titled *Land Measure*, *Medicine #1 and #2*, *Chemistry #1 and #2*, *Electric Machine*, and *Electric Arc*. The east wall contains eight murals titled *X-rays*, *Geology*, *Esoteric Symbol #1, 2, 3, 4, 5*, and *Operation*. On the south wall are five murals titled *Investigation*, *Cactácea*, *War*, *Science*, and *Researchers*. These murals that are located on the second level of the Ministry of Education all represent the diverse disciplines associated with science and technology in Mexico, such as medicine, chemistry, geology, and engineering.

The third level of the *Courtyard of Labor* consisted of 21 murals that were also divided into the north, east, and south walls. On the north wall Rivera painted seven panels titled *Music*, *Martyr David*, *Martyr Felipe Carrillo Puerto*, *Martyr Emiliano Zapata*, *Martyr Otilio Montaño*, *Dance*, and *Three Serpents*. The east wall consisted of seven panels titled *Tambourine Player*, *Deer Dance*, *Women with Vessel and Spoon*, *Fraternity*, *Women with Flowers and Vegetables*, *Painting*, and *Writing*. The south wall consisted of seven panels: *Serpents*, *Sculpture*, *The Three Graces*, *The Sciences*, *The Arts*, *Shells*, and *Architecture*.

In the second patio titled *Courtyard of the Fiestas*, there is a cycle of 24 panels that shows pleasant activities in Mexican culture like weddings, markets, folkloristic rituals, and festivals. When this section was in its production stage, de la Cueva, Guerrero, and Charlot were in charge of painting seven panels each. Rivera thought that the paintings were unsatisfactory. He destroyed most of the panels painted by his assistant artists and began to repaint the entire program himself. The four panels that Rivera did not destroy were *Washerwoman* and *Los Cargadores* (The Burden Carriers) by Charlot and *The Little Bull* and *Battle Dance* by de la Cueva. His assistants continued to help Rivera but began to work on less important aspects of the panels.

The images represented in the *Courtyard of the Fiestas* are on the first, second, and third levels of the south, west, and north walls of the Ministry of Education. On the first level of the south wall the titles of the panels are *Deer Dance*, *Corn Harvest*, *Corn Festival*, *Distribution of Land* (three connected panels), and *The Day of the Dead* #1, 2, and 3. The *Day of the Dead* panels portray a festival scene that is common in the Mexican culture. Rivera painted objects such as sugar molded skulls, *calacas* (skeletons), and masks, which represent the symbols of this practice. *The Day of the Dead* is not only a festival but a ritual that characterizes the way Mexicans embrace life and death as an integral part of their culture.

On the second level on the *Courtyard of Fiestas* there are 25 panels representing the various states in Mexico. The titles of the panels on the south wall are *Sinaloa-Sonora-Nayarit*, *Chihuahua*, *Coahuila*, *Nuevo León*, *Tamaulipas*, *Zacatecas*, *Aguascalientes*, *Guanajuato*, *Durango*, and *San Luis Potosi*. On the west wall there are six panels titled *Morelos-Querétaro*, *Hidalgo*, *Mexico*, *Jalisco*, *Colima*, and *Guerrero-Michoacán*. On the north wall there are nine panels titled *Tlaxcala*, *Puebla*, *Veracruz*, *Oaxaca*, *Chiapas*, *Tabasco*, *Campeche*, *Quintana Roo*, and *Yucatán*.

On the third floor of the *Courtyard of the Fiestas*, he depicted *corridos* or popular revolutionary songs. The cycle is composed of 26 panels that form two different themes: *Corrido de la Revolución Agraria* and *Corrido de la Revolución Proletaria*. The two themes illustrate the complex struggle that Mexico had been experiencing. Rivera used this opportunity to exalt the role of the workers and peasants that fought in the revolution, and to criticize the bourgeoisie as well as depict the downfall of capitalism. The *Corrido de la Revolución Proletaria* is located in the south wall and contains 10 panels titled *Distributing Arms*, *In the Trenches*, *The Wounded*, *"Let Him Work Who Wants to Eat,"* *The Cooperative*,

Death of the Capitalist, United Front, Our Bread, Protest, and *Emiliano Zapata.* Over the west and north walls is represented the *Corrido of the Agrarian Revolution.* There are 6 panels on the west wall titled *Singing the Corrido, To Work, Union, Learning the ABC's, Threshing,* and *Rain.* The north wall consists of 10 panels titled *Tractor, Capitalist Dinner, The Learned, Wall Street Banquet, Sleep-Night of the Poor, Fruits of the Earth, Orgy-Night of the Rich, "We Want to Work," Guarantees-Debris of Capitalism,* and *"All the World's Wealth Comes from the Land."*

In the panels titled *The Learned* and *Night of the Rich,* Rivera depicted a group of bourgeois intellectuals that in his view are unaware of the realities of Mexico. They are the philosopher and politician José Vasconcelos, his then-girlfriend author Antonieta Rivas Mercado, the poet José Juan Tablada, the subsecretary of education Ezequiel Chávez, and the famous Hindu poet Rabindranath Tagore. Vasconcelos is depicted sitting on a white elephant that represents his idealistic projects with his back against the viewer. Vasconcelos was one of the leading men responsible for the Mexican mural movement and the education of the masses. He was Rivera's sponsor in the commission of this great cycle of murals, but here Rivera represented him as a conservative and disgraced figure.

In the panels of the two patios, Rivera depicted a critical view of Mexico's history. In the stairwell, he represented more agrarian and social themes related to the triumph of the revolution. Rivera painted 11 panels that are titled *The Sea, The Littoral, The Diver, Tropical Mexico, Xochipilli and His Votaries, Plantation Serfdom, Peon, Highland Landscape, Mechanization of the Country, New World Schoolteacher,* and *Rivera and Associates.*

While Rivera worked on the Ministry of Education murals, he also began to work at the National Agricultural School at Chapingo in 1924. This school was the former Hacienda of Chapingo during the *Porfiriato* times and represented the social changes brought by the revolution. His assistants, de la Cueva, Guerrero, and Charlot, helped Rivera paint the Ministry of Education series while he began his third mural series in Chapingo. Both the Ministry of Education and the National Agricultural School murals portray the history of Mexico in different but complementary ways. The Ministry of Education murals, such as the *Corrido de la Revolución Proletaria,* portray the social and political story of the Mexican culture, while the National Agricultural School murals depict the agrarian struggle in Mexico.

At the National Agricultural School of Chapingo, Rivera incorporated the function of the school into the theme for his mural cycle. Rivera based his mural cycle on Emiliano Zapata's motto, "Here it is taught to exploit the land, not the man."[7] The mural program encompasses the entrance to the building, the chapel, the administrative building, and the entrance door to the chapel. The first sets of frescoes are located in the entrance staircase of the administrative building and illustrate the contrast between good and bad government. There are also scenes depicting the cultivation and harvesting of the land. In the chapel of the Agricultural School, Rivera depicted revolutionary martyrs integrated with agricultural scenes. The carved wooden entrance doors of the chapel illustrate contrasting scenes of the class struggle between the revolutionaries and the capitalists. Symbols such as the hammer and sickle and sheaves of corn are depicted on the entrance door and on the inside walls and ceiling of the chapel. Also in the chapel are some depictions of the earth through extraordinary female nudes that have a powerful expression.

In the chapel's altar, Rivera used his wife Lupe Marín to model the embodiment of nature. During this time, Marín was pregnant with their first child, Guadalupe, born in 1924. Rivera depicted Marín as a monumental pregnant nude woman who personified fertility in nature and the land. Two years later, Marín and Rivera had a second daughter, named Ruth. That same year, 1926, Rivera was to finish the mural at Chapingo, but he fell off of his ladder while working and was bedridden for three months. Soon after the accident and the arrival of Ruth, Rivera and Marín separated.

In April 1925, Rivera wrote a letter of resignation to the Communist Party officials because he wanted to devote himself to the Marxist movement through art. Rivera felt that his communist ideology would be better directed into painting than through militant activities. With the advice of Bertram Wolfe, Rivera decided to dedicate his entire time to the painting of murals. In July 1926, Rivera requested readmission to the Mexican Communist Party and was reinstated.

The two murals Rivera worked on during this time embodied the characteristics of Mexican muralism in the 1920s. The mural cycle in the Agricultural School at Chapingo was finished in 1926 with great acclaim. Rivera succeeded in depicting Mexican realism through his painting techniques, style, color, and themes. The mural series that Rivera depicted in the chapel of Chapingo was so impressive that art critics called it the Mexican Sistine Chapel.

In 1927, Rivera was invited by the Russian People's Commissar of Education, Anatoly Lunacharsky, to visit the Soviet Union. He was invited to attend as a guest painter for the 10th anniversary celebration of the October Revolution. Marín was not happy with the idea of Rivera leaving for Russia. Rivera later recalled, "I was, of course, delighted. Lupe was furious at the exaltation I showed, because I was going without her. It was about this time that our marriage began to fall apart."[8] Before he left for Russia, Rivera and Marín separated. The last words that Marín said to Rivera were, "Go to hell with your big-breasted girls!" While Rivera was in Russia, Lupe Marín married a mutual friend named Jorge Cuesta.

Before arriving in Russia, Rivera stayed for a few days in Berlin, where he gave an interview to a friend named Lotte Schwartz who was writing a book about his life. The book by Schwartz was published in 1928 as *Das Werk Diego Riveras*. While in Berlin, his friend Willie Muenzenberg invited him to hear Adolf Hitler speak. Rivera was astonished to see the mass of people gathered to hear Hitler speak and found Hitler to be a dangerous figure. He later reflected that there was something about Hitler that intrigued the German people. It was a kind of magnetism between him and the audience. Rivera sensed the fervor that Hitler evoked from the crowd that day and foresaw the strong influence he would have on the German people.

Rivera later told his friend Muenzenberg his thoughts and fears about Hitler and his power, but was not taken seriously. Some time later, Rivera's premonitions became a reality when his friend Muenzenberg and other fellow communists would be among the millions of human beings put to death by Hitler.

Rivera arrived in Moscow with Muenzenberg and Guadalupe Rodríguez, a friend from Mexico. Waiting for them at the train station was Soviet official Stanislav Peskovsky. Rivera was amazed by the processions of organized marching masses holding flags with a big red star and five picks. He later made several watercolor sketches of the processions, which were sold to Mrs. John D. Rockefeller Jr. One example of the images he painted is titled *May Day, Moscow* (1928). This series of paintings was executed in watercolors and depicted the crowds of people gathered to listen to Stalin speak.

Rivera also delivered lectures before the Congress of Friends of Russia and was named the Master of Monumental Painting by the Moscow School of Fine Arts. He was invited to a meeting at the Central Committee building to listen to the speech of the Soviet leader Joseph Stalin, who spoke about the October Revolution, its achievements, and its future purpose. During the speech, Rivera was sketching images of Stalin. When Stalin noticed, "he walked over and asked to see my pencil sketches. He examined all of them, selected one, and wrote on the back of it in blue pencil: 'Greetings to the Mexican revolutionaries,' and signed 'Stalin.'"[9] Rivera was invited by Commissar of Education Anatoly Lunacharsky to paint a mural in the Red Army Club, but after some disagreements and obscure intrigues by some artists and government officers, the commissar requested that Rivera return to Mexico. Thus, the mural of the Red Army Club was never painted.

Rivera returned to Mexico in June 1928 and was immediately commissioned to design the scenes, props, and costumes for a ballet titled *H.P.*, which is an abbreviation for horsepower. This anti-imperialist ballet, composed by the Mexican musician Carlos Chávez, has a plot that illustrates the capitalistic exploitation of Latin America by the United States and its fateful result—the revolt and triumph of worker over capitalist. The ballet *H.P.* was first performed at the Philadelphia Academy of Music with Leopold Stokowski conducting in 1932. Rivera also created an album of the costumes that was purchased by Mrs. John D. Rockefeller Jr. and later donated to the Museum of Modern Art in New York. Rivera enjoyed working on the ballet production but found it to be a substantial amount of work that distracted him from his main passion: mural painting.

According to some sources, in July 1928 Rivera met Frida Kahlo at a party hosted by Tina Modotti. Modotti was an Italian photographer and a member of the Mexican Communist Party who moved in the same artistic and political circles as Rivera and Kahlo. At the party, Kahlo invited Rivera to her house in Coyoacán to view her paintings. Rivera immediately recognized Kahlo's name as a young girl who had

Diego Rivera and Frida Kahlo with Frances Flynn Paine and Mrs. William C. Hammer in Philadelphia working on the design of the ballet Horse Power, *1932. (AP Photo)*

studied at the National Preparatory School, and who had made jokes about him when he was painting there. Another version of the story says that Frida visited him at the Ministry of Education to show him her artwork. What is known for sure is that Rivera went to Kahlo's house in June 1928 and soon after the two began dating. On August 21, 1929, Rivera and Kahlo were married in a civil ceremony by the Mayor of Coyoácan. Kahlo later remembered,

> At seventeen [twenty] I fell in love with Diego, and my (parents) did not like this because Diego was a Communist and because they said that he looked like a fat, fat, fat Brueghel. Nevertheless, I arranged everything in the court of Coyoacán so that we could be married the 21st of August, 1929. No one went to the wedding, only my father, who said to Diego, "Notice that my daughter is a sick person and all her life she will be sick; she is intelligent,

but not pretty. Think it over if you want, and if you wish to get married, I give you my permission."[10]

In April 1929, Rivera had been appointed director of the Academy of San Carlos. Rivera proposed a change in curriculum that combined eight years of daytime factory work with art courses at night. He also advised that students receive day and night art courses to further reinforce the knowledge learned through practical experience. Rivera's curriculum suggestions received criticism from the administration. The most contentious proposition made by Rivera was to join the Academy of San Carlos with the National School of Architecture. On May 10, 1930, Rivera was forced to resign as director of the Academy of San Carlos.

In September 1929, Rivera was expelled from the Communist Party for "disobedience to its policies" in spite of his dedicated efforts to defend Tina Modotti, a radical communist activist, from the accusations of the Mexican government.

Also in this same year, he began the mural titled *The History of Mexico*. The mural was commissioned by the central government and was located in the National Palace in Mexico City, on the wall of the main stairway. Rivera incorporated the architectural structure of the stairway into his theme, using the movement of the stairway to connect each part of the mural's storyline. Rivera divided the staircase wall into three sections. The center wall depicted the Spanish Conquest of Mexico in 1519–1521, the colonial period from 1521 to 1821, the American invasion of 1846–1848, the Reform Period of 1855–1862, the French invasion of 1862–1867, the *Porfiriato* from 1876 to 1910, the Mexican Revolution from 1910 to 1920, and the first two revolutionary governments until 1930. In the two adjoining walls, Rivera depicted the pre-Columbian world and modern-day Mexico.

Rivera's mural at the National Palace is a didactic narrative of the *history of Mexico* and represents, in the words of scholar Desmond Rochfort, the "reality unhindered by the trappings of contemporary moral or political assertions."[11] Rivera incorporated images and symbols of ancient Mesoamerican civilizations and the process of *mestizaje* to express the political and social struggles in Mexico at that time and to explore issues of Mexican identity. Rivera also juxtaposed these three ideas and depicted, through a profusion of figures and details, a nationalistic theme in which he presents the ancient civilizations as the true answer for Mexico.

Also in 1929, a short time after Rivera began the mural at the National Palace, he was commissioned by the American ambassador to Mexico, Dwight Morrow, to paint a mural at the Cortés Palace in the city of Cuernavaca. Rivera was asked to paint the mural in Cuernavaca as a gesture of goodwill by Morrow to the people of Cuernavaca, and an attempt to clean his political image after his involvement in some obscure U.S. foreign policy deals that had negatively affected Mexico. The mural at Cuernavaca consisted of three walls located on the second floor of an outdoor corridor of the 16th-century palace. Rivera decided to depict the theme of *The History of Cuernavaca and Morelos* from the pre-Columbian times to the revolution of 1910.

The mural was constructed in a chronological sequence running from right to left of the corridor's walls. The mural used symbols and metaphors to narrate the history of the Aztec resistance, the Spanish conquest of Cuernavaca, and the colonial society. Rivera chose to juxtapose the past and present history of Mexico as a reflection on the identity of his nation.

The murals of Diego Rivera in the 1920s started in the National Preparatory School with impassioned idealism, but a hesitant ideological agenda. The social and political events emanating from the turmoil of the revolution and the developments in Mexico during that decade motivated the emergence in his works of the themes of revolution, the land, and the cultural traditions of the people.

By the end of the 1920s, besides the cultural focus in the local and immediate concerns of the revolution, Rivera's murals accomplished an interrogation of the historical experience and a redefinition of the Mexican national identity in the light of the periods of independence and revolution.

NOTES

1. Desmond Rochfort, *Mexican Muralists* (New York: Chronicle Books, 1993), 21.

2. Antonio Rodríguez, *A History of Mexican Mural Painting* (London: Thames and Hudson, 1969), 186.

3. Ibid.

4. Bertram D. Wolfe, *The Fabulous Life of Diego Rivera* (New York: Cooper Square Press, 1963), 152.

5. Ibid., 153.

6. Ibid., 142.

7. Rochfort, *Mexican Muralism*, 67.

8. Diego Rivera with Gladys March, *My Art, My Life: An Autobiography* (New York: Dover, 1991), 83.

9. Ibid., 91.

10. Hayden Herrera, *Frida: A Biography of Frida Kahlo* (New York: Perennial, 2002), 99.

11. Rochfort, *Mexican Muralists*, 85. Soon after meeting, Rivera and Marín married in Guadalajara and moved close to the Zocalo (Central Plaza) in Mexico City.

Chapter 4

RIVERA IN THE UNITED STATES (1930–1933)

With several murals completed in Mexico, Diego Rivera was commissioned to paint his first mural in the United States. In 1926, he received an invitation by William Gerstle, the president of the San Francisco Art Commission, to paint a mural in the California School of Fine Arts (San Francisco Art Institute). Rivera later accepted this commission along with another mural to be painted at the San Francisco Stock Exchange. This second mural was commissioned by the building's architect, Timothy Pflueger, by recommendation of the sculptor Ralph Stackpole. Pflueger offered Rivera $2,500 for the Stock Exchange mural and Gerstle proposed a payment to Rivera of $1,500 for the mural at the San Francisco Art Institute. Rivera accepted both offers and, after much effort to obtain a visa, both Rivera and Frida Kahlo arrived in San Francisco in 1930.

When Rivera and Kahlo arrived in San Francisco, they were greeted with much enthusiasm by Pflueger and Stackpole. They moved into Stackpole's studio in an artist district located on Montgomery Street. Soon after their arrival, Rivera and Kahlo ran into Edward Weston. Weston was an American photographer who had lived in Mexico with Tina Modotti, a mutual friend of Rivera and Kahlo. Weston wrote in his diary on December 14, 1930:

> I met Diego! I stood beside a stone block, stepped out as he lumbered downstairs into Ralph's courtyard on Jessop Place—and he took me clear off my feet in an embrace. I photographed Diego again, his new wife—Frida—too; she is sharp contrast to Lupe, petite—a little doll alongside Diego, but a doll in size only, for she is strong and quite beautiful, shows very little of her father's German blood. Dressed in native costume even to *huaraches*, she causes much excitement on the streets of San Francisco. People stop in their tracks to look in wonder. We ate at a little Italian restaurant where many of the artists gather, recalled the old days in Mexico, with promises of meeting again in Carmel.[1]

Frida Kahlo dressed in traditional Mexican clothing and captured the attention of everyone. She had such a distinct and fascinating style that eventually fashion magazines all over the world would imitate it.

However, the arrival of Diego Rivera in San Francisco was received with skepticism and ethnic stereotypes by the journalists, as was typical of the time. He was viewed as a Mexican peasant of "rustic normality" and his body gestures, clothes, and speech were presented as inferior.[2] Journalists described him as a disheveled Mexican peasant and they were incapable of recognizing that a Mexican artist could be better than any American artist of the time. More sophisticated critics reacted with prejudice to his political message, describing the Mexican artist as "a political propagandist, not a painter; that he portrayed a false image of Mexico as an idealized pre-Columbian land, distracting the attention of the audience to not see the extreme poverty of the country; a nationalist, leftist thinker who painted murals with class imagery not appropriate for a country like the United States, where supposedly there were no class divisions and everybody lived under the protection of social and civil rights."[3]

The controversies continued and the reporters and diverse artists attacked the patrons of the murals, saying that they were favoring a foreign artist to the detriment of the local artists of California. They criticized Timothy Pflueger, representing him in caricatures as a "Communist General" or a "Soviet Farm Commissar" with a tyrannical attitude, exploiting his soldiers and workers. Pflueger and Stackpole had invited some Californian artists—Ruth Cravath, Adeline Kent, Robert Howard, Clifford Wight, Arthur Putnam, and Otis Oldfield—to paint some of the interior walls of the building as a complement to Rivera's main mural. The artists that were chosen were familiar with Rivera's method and style, but Ray Boynton and Maynard Dixon, the most prominent muralists in the city, resented being left out. Dixon noted bitterly, "The Stock Exchange could look the world over without finding a man more inappropriate for the part than Rivera. He is a professed Communist and has publicly caricatured American financial institutions." To add fire to the situation, William R. Hearst, the powerful newspaper tycoon declared, "Rivera is not qualified on account of his communist tendencies."[4]

Two months after Rivera and Kahlo had arrived in California, and in the middle of this debate about his talents and qualifications, Rivera began to work on the mural at the San Francisco Stock Exchange. He was given the center wall, which was located in the interior staircase of the Stock Exchange's Luncheon Club and measured 44 square feet. The mural, titled *Allegory of California,* was a romantic representation of modernity in American Society. Rivera depicted symbolic images that embodied California's natural resources as well as the contributions of its people. The art critic Emily Joseph stated:

> The significance of the Californian mural is plain. The heroic figure of California, the mother, the giver is dominant. She gives gold and fruit and grain. California and her riches are here for all. Without the genius of her own sons, her riches would be a dead matter. Under the earth, over the earth, and above the earth, man's will and spirit transform gold, wood, metal into gods that are to liberate the life of man. The idea of liberation is involved in the entire fresco.[5]

In the mural, modern California is represented by the portrait of the famous and popular tennis player Helen Wills Moody, who displays vitality and strength. Her right hand digs the earth to obtain its subterranean riches, while her left hand holds the plentiful natural products that grow in its surface. This is an artistic metaphor for the abundant resources of California such as fruit, oil, gold, and the sun. Below appear the portraits of the renowned horticulturalist Luther Burbank, and also James Marshall, who discovered gold at Sutter's mill in 1848 and precipitated the Gold Rush. Also included in the scene are an engineer, a worker, and a farmer, all symbols of the exploitation of the natural resources and of creative human efforts. A young man with a model airplane represents the future and the dreams of progress of modern society. In the upper part of the mural, the shipping and oil industries, pillars of California economy, are depicted. Through these images, Rivera represented California as a dynamic and progressive land with a great industrial power, embracing the future opportunities that modernism could bring.

Rivera completed the mural at the San Francisco Stock Exchange in February 1931 and began his second mural at the San Francisco Art Institute in June of that same year. Rivera's contract with William Gerstle stated that he was to paint a small wall that measured 120 square feet at the School of Fine Arts. Rivera felt that the proposed wall was not suitable for the mural he planned and asked for a larger wall. Rivera was given a larger wall with the expectation that his pay would stay the same. Rivera accepted the offer and began to paint the mural, titled *The Making of a Fresco* (1931).

The subject of this mural was the vitality of American industrial life. Like his first mural at the Stock Exchange, he painted the positive attributes that modernism had on society in the beginning of the 20th century. The fresco is divided in six sections by a wooden scaffold that produces the illusion of a three-dimensional space. This is a fresco within a fresco that shows the building of a modern industrial city. In the center of the mural, Rivera depicted himself sitting on the scaffold painting with his assistants, Clifford Wight and Matthew Barnes, along with the gigantic image of a construction worker that has a medal with a red star in his breast pocket, the symbol of Soviet socialism. Rivera emphasized the fundamental role of the workers in the construction of the material wealth of modern society. On both sides of the mural, Rivera painted diverse aspects of industrialization. Depictions of men constructing a high-rise building and factory workers in the assembly line represented the prosperous future. On the ground below Rivera are architect Timothy Pflueger, the designer of the San Francisco Stock Exchange, William Gerstle (the president of the San Francisco Art Association who commissioned the mural), and architect Arthur Brown, Jr., who designed the school's new building, as well as other important landmarks of the city, such as the Coit Tower and the City Hall. These three persons appear in the role of patrons as in the medieval and Renaissance traditions in painting.

On the left partition of the mural can be seen the sculptor Ralph Stackpole and the artist Clifford Wight at work, in the company of two laborers. On the right side, there is a drafting table with three figures: architect Michael Goodman, architect Geraldine Colby Frickie, and engineer Albert Barrows, who worked in the firm of Timothy Pflueger. They appear in the design and construction of the city, while above them are a group of workers actually building a skyscraper. The self-portrait of Rivera's back, showing his fat buttocks to the audience, was considered by some people as a gesture of mockery and insult, although Rivera's actual intention is unknown.

While Rivera was working in San Francisco, he received a letter from the president of Mexico, Pascual Ortiz Rubio, who insisted that Rivera return to Mexico and finish the mural at the National Palace. With the help of Gerstle, a member of the board of the California School of Fine Arts, Rivera was able to stay in San Francisco until he finished the mural, after which both Rivera and Kahlo returned to Mexico.

Although Rivera had left two assistants painting the mural at the National Palace, he was unhappy with their work and repainted it himself. While working on the mural, he was visited by a New York art dealer named Frances Flynn Paine. Paine invited Rivera to participate in an exhibition at the Metropolitan Museum in New York. After finishing the main wall of the stairway at the National Palace three and a half months later, Rivera began to prepare for his one-man show in New York. In November 1931, Rivera, Kahlo, and Paine sailed for New York.

When they arrived, Rivera immediately began to work on his solo exhibition in his new studio located in the New York Museum of Modern Art, which Paine had provided. Rivera worked on seven movable murals for the show, four of which were altered versions of previous murals he had done in Mexico. The remaining three were depictions of New York City life, including images of industrial workers, power plants, the construction of the Rockefeller Center, and the Great Depression. The exhibition also included 150 paintings that varied in media such as pastel, oil, and watercolor. Rivera's solo art exhibition in New York incorporated all of his art periods as a painter, from realism to muralism.

The New York exhibition was a great success, although it failed to satisfy Rivera's expectations. Rivera felt that he was unsuccessful in illustrating the essence of mural paintings to the American art world. He wanted North Americans to understand the functionality of painting murals, but discovered that their "preference for commodities of easy manipulation" would not allow them to fully comprehend the murals' intended purpose. Rivera was disappointed that he was not able to convey the spirit and purpose that muralism had in Mexico.

In April 1932, Diego Rivera and Frida Kahlo arrived in Detroit, Michigan, to begin a mural at the Detroit Institute of Art. Rivera had been commissioned by William Valentiner, the director, and Edgar Richardson, curator of education, a year earlier while working on the murals in California. Rivera received the invitation letter from Valentiner, which stated:

> The Arts Commission decided to ask you to help us beautify the museum and give fame to its hall through your great work. . . . The Arts Commission will be very glad to have your suggestions of the motifs, which could be selected after you are here. They would be pleased if you could possibly find something out of the history of Detroit, or some motif suggesting the developing of industry in this town; but at the end they decided to leave it entirely to you, what you think best to do.[6]

With the artistic freedom given to Rivera for the next mural, he began to research immediately.

About a month before Rivera's arrival in Detroit, some 4,000 laid-off workers demonstrated against the Ford Motor Company in Dearborn, Michigan, demanding fair compensation and denouncing repressive treatment. It was initially a peaceful march, but as the workers were approaching the factory, Dearborn police and firemen threw tear gas and hit them with jets of water. At the same time some members of the police and Ford's guards fired hundreds of shots, killing 5 workers and leaving more than 20 wounded. This situation illustrated the economic and social tensions building up in the United States during the years of the Great Depression.

In Detroit, Rivera and Kahlo stayed at the Brevoort Hotel, conveniently located in front of the Institute of Art. Rivera was originally commissioned to paint two walls, each of which measured 50 square yards, for the amount of $10,000, but after reviewing the mural space, he requested four walls located in a garden court. Edsel Ford, who was the chairman of the Arts Commission and donor for the mural, accepted Rivera's request and raised his pay to $25,000 after seeing his preliminary plans and research.

Rivera prepared for the mural by studying the city's local landscape, factories, and culture. Rivera was also invited to the museum of machinery in Dearborn, where he met Henry Ford. In Dearborn, and more precisely in the Rouge plant of Ford Motor Company, he stayed long into the night studying all the machinery that had fascinated him since he was a child in Guanajuato. It took him three months of conceptual exploration in which he took hundreds of notes and made sketches and studies for the various scenes he was contemplating. Rivera and his assistants also visited other factories, such as Chrysler Motor Company, Parke-Davis Chemical, Michigan Alkali Plant, Detroit Edison, and the Detroit Chemical Factory. He also benefited from the many photographs taken by Ford staff photographer W. J. Stettler in those industrial complexes. After dedicating long hours to examining the city and the industrial centers, Rivera created preliminary drawings of possible subject matter for the mural. These sketches were presented to Edsel Ford and approved with the inclusion of images of other factories in Detroit besides the automobile industry. With Ford's approval, Rivera began to work on his next mural project, titled *Detroit Industry*.

The mural cycle that Rivera envisioned consisted of 27 panels with the theme of the evolution of technology. He counted on a good team of assistants, the majority of whom had worked with him in San Francisco, that included Clifford Wight, Lord Hastings (a British aristocrat of socialist ideas), Ernst Halberstadt, Andrés Sánchez-Flores (chemist), Arthur Niendorf, Lucienne Bloch, and Stephen Dimitroff. The challenge was paramount and the team worked around the clock. The walls required five layers of plaster that needed to be prepared with utmost precision to ensure long-term survival. With this team and with Rivera himself painting 15 hours a day, the set of murals was completed in only eight months.

The cycle *Detroit Industry* is an artistic representation of the interaction of science, technology, and human life. It highlights the infinite possibilities of creativity in producing a modern progressive world to serve and not to alienate people. The panels of the north and south walls depict the manufacturing operations for the new Model T produced by the Ford Motor Company. In the north wall can be seen the semiautomated production line for the V-8 engines with monoblock assembly, iron and steel production in furnaces, the metal foundry process to make part moulds, the representation of the indigenous American and black races with monumental figures, and smaller images, the *Manufacture of Poisonous Gas* and *Vaccination*, in which Rivera used the recently kidnapped child of Charles Lindbergh as a model. Finally, there are illustrations of a healthy human embryo and cells damaged by intoxication.

On the south wall appears Rivera's rendition of the production of transmissions, final assembly of the chassis and car body, and the Pressed Steel Building operations, in which the big stamping press machine resembles in its silhouette the Aztec statue, the mother-earth goddess Coatlicue. Rivera wanted to establish a parallel here between the creative power of the goddess to produce life and the creative function of the stamping press to produce formed pieces, both requiring in return human sacrifice in the form of labor or death. In addition there are also monumental renditions of the white and Asian races and smaller panels referring to the pharmaceutical and commercial chemical industries, as well as surgery and geological elements. On the east wall there are images of women holding grains and fruits, as well as a baby in the bulb of a plant. On the west wall are found images titled *Aviation* and *Interdependence of North and South.*[7]

In completing the monumental work of creating these 27 panels, Rivera also had to deal with several unexpected complications. The first one was the Italian baroque style structure of the building itself. The modern motifs that he planned to paint on the walls of the institute did not harmonize with the ornate architecture. He resolved the problem by overpowering the architecture instead of trying to integrate it into his theme. Rivera achieved this by creating monumental depictions of the modern industries from the Detroit area that would attract the main attention of the viewers. Thus, agriculture, chemistry, medicine, airplane, and automobile industries were all part of Rivera's mural cycle. The various subject matters taken from the surroundings of Detroit proved to strengthen the mural.

In spite of his largely optimistic and uncritical view of the modern American industrial production, the second complication Rivera faced was bitter criticism centered on images that resembled religious iconography. Reverend Ralph Higgins, a local Episcopalian church leader, criticized Rivera for images that, in Higgins's interpretation, represented the Holy Family. In the *Vaccination* panel, Rivera depicted a child in the arms of a nurse while being vaccinated by a physician next to a horse, a cow, and a sheep, symbolic representations of vaccines that are taken from these animal tissues. Reverend Higgins was not convinced of Rivera's portrayal, however, and generated controversy in identifying Rivera's composition showing the animals and the three persons as a sacrilegious reference to the biblical passage of the Nativity.[8] Soon after, a columnist visited Rivera to question his artistic motifs. Even if the connection between the personages in *Vaccination* and in the story of the Nativity had been established intentionally by Rivera, he maintained that the image was not heretical or even disrespectful at all.

The third complication came in July 1932, when Frida Kahlo suffered a miscarriage while in Detroit. Seven years earlier, in 1925, Kahlo had been involved in a bus accident that left her pelvis, left arm, and spinal column fractured. More tragic than her multiple fractures was the iron rod that had entered through her abdomen and vagina and pierced her pelvis. This made it difficult if not impossible for Kahlo to give birth. Although she understood the consequences, she always dreamed of bearing a child and got pregnant several times. While in

Detroit, she miscarried and was sent to the Henry Ford Hospital. She recovered slowly and fell into a deep depression afterwards.

Two months later, she was given the news that her mother was ill. Kahlo traveled to Mexico City while Rivera continued to paint in Detroit. Rivera worked 18-hour days while Kahlo was in Mexico. He became fatigued with the stress of his wife's miscarriage and then absence, the criticism of his painting, and the long working hours that left him little time for eating. When Kahlo returned to Detroit after her mother's death, she found Rivera significantly thinner.

When Rivera finished the mural at the Detroit Institute of Art, the museum held an exclusive opening for the art patrons of Detroit before opening for the general public. The local art patrons were unhappy with the mural, expressing dissatisfaction with the loss of serenity that the garden had before the mural was painted there. Rivera reacted against the accusation of destroying the garden with irony: "The loss of the peaceful, lovely garden, which had been like an oasis in the industrial desert of Detroit. Thanks to me, their charming sanctum was now an epitome of everything that made noise and smoke and dust."[9] Although Rivera was disappointed with the patrons' response, he reminded them that the subject of the mural was the reason why they were wealthy.

A few days after the patrons viewed the mural, a group of engineers and workers in the steel and automobile factories in Detroit visited the museum, led by an engineer of the Chrysler automobile factory. The group of men favored the mural for its realistic depictions of the mechanical functions and workers from various factories also visited the museum to express their gratitude for the dignified representation of the working class. Their approval provided security for the mural, which had been threatened with destruction. Soon after all this controversy, Edsel Ford publicly announced his support and satisfaction with the mural. The art institute director, Valentiner, also confidently declared, "I am thoroughly convinced the day will come when Detroit will be proud to have this work in its midst. In the years to come they will be ranked among the truly great art treasures of America."[10] He was correct and the murals solidified Rivera's fame in the United States.

Rivera was ultimately pleased with the positive response and stated that the overwhelming approval of his mural by the Detroit workers was the beginning of the realization of his life's dream.

The Detroit murals showed Rivera's passion for industrial design, his intuitive knowledge of modern technology, and his understanding of ancient cultures. Their significance lies in the depiction of the relationship between biology and technology, as was Rivera's intention. Rivera presented the challenge for the future as finding the right balance that may assure human survival.

While Rivera was working on the mural in Detroit, he was visited by Raymond Hood, the architect for the RCA building in New York. At the request of Nelson Rockefeller, Hood invited Rivera, Pablo Picasso, and Henry Matisse to each submit a draft for the mural in the RCA that he was commissioning. The rules of the competition imposed certain restrictions on the artist, such as the stipulation that the work be monochromatic and decorative. Matisse rejected the offer, arguing that his work was not compatible with the space of the building, and Picasso declined abruptly, disagreeing with the imposed conditions. Rivera initially refused the invitation, explaining that his career was at a level of recognition in which competitions were offensive for him, but he eventually entered into tense negotiations for the commission. Hood wanted Rivera to paint a decorative mural that encompassed an American theme, while Rivera wanted to create a mural that amplified the architecture and had expressive or symbolic power.

Finally, Rivera accepted the commission, but only through the personal intervention of Nelson Rockefeller and the assurance that he would be allowed to paint a mural in color and with a narrative. Rivera submitted his designs in January 1933 and Hood commissioned Rivera to paint a 1,000-square-foot wall on behalf of Rockefeller for the sum of $21,000. Rivera went to New York a month later to see the location of the mural and presented Hood with a second set of proposed designs with some modifications.

Rockefeller set a very precise theme for the mural: *The Man at the Crossroads Looking with Hope and High Vision to the Choosing of a New and Better Future*. He wanted to include philosophical and spiritual content that would make people stop and think, stimulating a spiritual awakening. The mural intended to depict the social, political, industrial, and scientific possibilities of the 20th century. Ultimately, the mural would help in the comprehension of the meaning and mystery of life.

Rivera began painting the RCA mural in March 1933, the same month that he finished the mural in Detroit. The New York mural, more commonly known as *Man at the Crossroads*, was located in front of the main entrance of the building above the elevator. The scaffold, traced sketches, wet wall, and colors had all been prepared by Rivera's assistants a month before he began his work. His team of assistants included Ben Shahn, Lucienne Bloch, Stephen Dimitroff, Hideo Noda, Lou Block, Arthur Niendorf, and Antonio Sánchez Flores. Rivera began painting with little interruption, although some of the architects and engineers were uneasy with images that they defined as too realistic and aggressive. Rivera received a letter from Rockefeller, however, expressing that he had seen a photograph of the work in the news-

Diego Rivera painting at Rockefeller Center, 1933. (AP Photo)

paper and was pleased with the images and wanted Rivera to finish by the first of May, the date set for the public opening.

During this time, the world was going through social and political turmoil. The United States was in the midst of the Great Depression under the leadership of Franklin D. Roosevelt, and Adolf Hitler came into power as chancellor of Germany. The social and economic instability that Rivera witnessed and experienced while in New York inspired him to express his response to those international political events in his mural. The mural's ambitious title, *Man at the Crossroads Looking for Hope and High Vision to the Choosing of a New and Better Future*, proved to correspond to the historical times.

Rivera also continued to paint subject matter that represented modern technology and its consequences. The left part of the mural represented the capitalistic world, which Rivera depicted in the context of human evolution. He depicted humans with the ability to gain enlightenment through the control of the forces of nature and create science and technology. In his view this process was destined to replace the superstitions of the past.

This section of the mural also depicts Charles Darwin proposing the theory of human evolution from the apes. The image of a monkey holding hands with a baby generated controversy because some critics felt that Rivera was disrespecting the image of the infant Jesus and denying God's creation of man. Rivera also presented here the poor and homeless being repressed by the police in the streets while a group of rich individuals are playing cards and dancing in a party. There is also an image showing the militaristic tendency of the social system, with a group of children of diverse ethnicities being taught by an Anglo-American teacher to interpret the world seen through a huge magnifying glass with the bias of the capitalistic culture.

On the opposite section of the mural, Rivera portrayed the socialist world in the context of the development of the technical power of man. The panel depicts a crumbling statue of Caesar that symbolizes the end of tyranny while workers are shown thriving off the land.

In this part, there are depictions of the practice of sports in the socialist society and the masses defending their civil rights. Also Rivera shows people of all ages and professions being educated by teachers like Leon Trotsky, Friedrich Engels, and Karl Marx. As a consequence, they are seeing the world through the lens of the socialist system: "Workers of the World Unite!"

Monumental images of a telescope, a microscope, machines, outer space, atoms, and nature were just some of the images depicting the advancement of man through science, technology, and philosophy. At the center of the mural Rivera painted a "telescope that brings to the vision and knowledge of man the most remote celestial bodies. The microscope makes visible and comprehensible to man infinitesimal living organisms, connecting atoms and cells with the astral system."[11] A dignified worker is controlling a machine that receives cosmic energy and transforms it into productive energy. At the same time, a large hand comes from the entrails of the machine and is holding a crystal sphere. Emerging from the sphere are the sciences, such as biology, medicine, astronomy, physics, and chemistry, represented with atoms, viruses, bacterium, parts of the body, division of cells, and the dynamics of celestial bodies within space. Rivera explained the representation of man in this section. The center panel focuses on man's ability to transform natural goods that the earth produces. Man appears as a peasant that plants the seeds, a worker that transforms the raw materials, and a soldier that represents sacrifice. Man depicted in his triple aspect is responsible for creating an optimistic vision of balance and hope.

He also included an image of Vladimir Lenin holding hands with both a black American and a white Russian soldier, symbolizing the unification and solidarity of future nations. This image contrasts sharply with the rich people on the mural's other side, who are indulging in frivolous and vicious activities of no social significance. Images of juxtaposing the excess of wealth with war and unemployment were all part of this fresco, which clearly had a communist orientation, supporting the idea of capitalism's eventual fall through the unavoidable socialist transformation of society.

Before May, Rivera had received only enthusiastic opinions of his mural from the Rockefeller family. On May 4, however, Rivera received a letter from Nelson Rockefeller stating,

> While I was in the No.1 building at Rockefeller Center yesterday viewing the progress of your thrilling mural, I noticed that

in the most recent portion of the painting you had included a portrait of Lenin. This piece is beautifully painted, but it seems to me that his portrait, appearing in this mural, might very easily seriously offend a great many people. If it were in a private house it would be one thing, but this mural is in a public building and the situation is therefore quite different. As much as I dislike to do so, I am afraid we must ask you to substitute the face of some unknown man where Lenin's face now appears. . . . I am sure you will understand our feeling in this situation and we will greatly appreciate your making the suggested substitution.[12]

Upon reading the Rockefeller letter, Rivera sought the advice of his friends about this matter. Rivera was conflicted over Rockefeller's suggestion and felt that for him to remove Lenin from the mural would result in one demand after another until his artistic expression would be destroyed. On May 6, Rivera sent Nelson Rockefeller the following answer:

In reply to your kind letter of May 4. 1933, I wish to tell you my actual feelings on the matters you raise, after I have given considerable reflection to them. The head of Lenin was included in the original sketch now in the hands of Mr. Raymond Hood, and in the drawings in line made on the wall at the beginning of my work. Each time it appeared as a general and abstract representation of the concept of leader, an indispensable human figure.

I should like, as far as possible, to find an acceptable solution to the problem you raise, and suggest that I could change the sector which shows society people playing bridge and dancing, and put in its place in perfect balance with the Lenin portion, a figure of some great American historical leader, such as Lincoln, who symbolizes the unification of the country and the abolition of slavery, surrounded by John Brown, Nat Turner, William Lloyd Garrison or Wendell Phillips and Harriet Beecher Stowe, and perhaps some scientific figure like McCormick, inventor of McCormick reaper, which aided in the victory of anti-slavery forces by providing sufficient wheat to sustain the Northern armies.

> I am sure that the solution I propose will entirely clarify the historical meaning of the figure of leader as represented by Lenin and Lincoln, and no one will be able to object to them without objecting to the most fundamental feelings of human love and solidarity and the constructive social force represented by such men. Also, it will clarify the general meaning of the painting.[13]

On May 9, just three days after Rivera sent the letter to Rockefeller, Rivera went into work and noticed the presence of policemen patrolling the RCA building. As the day progressed, the building was progressively cleared out with the exception of Rivera and his assistants. A man by the name of Todd Robertson came into the RCA building and gave Rivera the ultimatum of omitting Lenin's image. Rivera declined and Mr. Robertson ordered him to stop, gave him his last paycheck of $14,000, and escorted him out of the building. While all of this was transpiring, a group of workers came in with a stretched canvas and covered the mural. The next day the entrance of the building was closed off with a large curtain to block any view of the mural.

Beginning the same day and for the next several days, demonstrations of people gathered around the RCA building. Many artists, writers, and art lovers defended Rivera and expressed their opposition to Rockefeller's decision. Although there were many patrons who supported Rivera, this controversy proved damaging to his future work in the United States. On May 12 Rivera received a telegram from Albert Kahn, architect for the General Motors World's Fair at Chicago, which stated that he had "instructions from General Motors executives (to) discontinue with (the) Chicago mural."[14] That same day, the Rockefellers were quoted in an article in the *New York World-Telegram* that stated, "The uncompleted fresco of Diego Rivera will not be destroyed, nor in any way mutilated, but . . . will be covered, to remain hidden for an indefinite time."[15] In February 1934, six months after the Rockefellers' statement, Rivera's mural was smashed to pieces.

The mural in New York proved to be one of the most controversial undertakings in Rivera's life. His partnership with one of the most powerful and wealthy families in the United States became just as important as the painting itself. Due to the negative press and the influence the Rockefeller family had, Rivera was not allowed to paint in the United States for some time. His reputation as a communist created problems, but Rivera continued to stand by his beliefs. The mural *Man at the Crossroads* in the RCA building would not be seen by the public, other than in a photograph that was taken secretly by his assistant Lucienne Bloch. A year later he would re-create the mural in Mexico (see photo on page 69 in chapter 5).

Before leaving New York in the second half of 1933, Rivera painted a series of 21 portable panels with the title *Portrait of America* for the New Workers' School. The panels are titled *Colonial America, The American Revolution, Revolution and Reaction: Shay's Rebellion, Expansion, The Conflict over Slavery, The Civil War, Reconstruction, The Labor Movement, Class War, Modern Industry, World War, The New Freedom, Imperialism, Depression, The "New Deal," Division and Depression,*

Diego Rivera painting a mural at the New Workers' School, 1933. (Library of Congress)

Mussolini, *Opponent of Fascism*, *Proletarian Unity*, *Opponent of Nazism*, and *Hitler*.

The theme of this mural cycle is the history of the United States and it shows the great ability and passion that Rivera had to interpret history. Impressive are the beauty and vibrancy of the portraits of figures such as Benjamin Franklin, Thomas Paine, Abraham Lincoln, Ralph Waldo Emerson, Henry David Thoreau, Walt Whitman, J.P. Morgan, and others. As friend and biographer Bertram Wolfe noted of Rivera, "Many may disagree with his interpretation of our history, but none can deny its impact or its strength. . . . Indeed, whatever its shortcomings of propagandistic onesidedness, there is no example by one of our own painters that comes anywhere near giving so moving a portrayal of our people, our history, and our land."[16]

The New Workers' School closed down in 1966, but the multipanel mural had been donated to the Ladies' Garment Union of New York in 1941. Later that year, the panels were moved to the Ladies' Garment Union's Recreation Center (Camp Unity) in Forest Park, Pennsylvania. Only 13 panels were installed because the other 8, including the largest one, *Communist Unity*, were considered too controversial and were discarded by some of the union officers, ending later in the hands of private collectors in Mexico (4), Venezuela (1), Sweden (1), and the United States (2). Unfortunately, the 13 panels remaining at Camp Unity in Pennsylvania were destroyed by fire in 1969.

NOTES

1. Edward Weston, *The Daybooks of Edward Weston* (Millerton, NY: An Aperture Book, 1961), 1:198–99.

2. Anthony W. Lee, *Painting on the Left: Diego Rivera, Radical Politics, and San Francisco's Public Murals* (Berkeley: University of California Press, 1999), 57–58.

3. Ibid.

4. Ibid., 62–64.

5. Emily Joseph, "'Rivera Murals in San Francisco," *Creative Art*, May 1931.

6. Letter to Rivera from Valentiner dated April 27, 1931, Detroit Institute of Arts Archives.

7. Linda Bank Downs, *Diego Rivera: The Detroit Industry Murals* (Detroit: Detroit Institute of Arts, 1999), 65–146; Dorothy McMeekin, *Diego Rivera: Science and Creativity in the Detroit Murals* (Detroit: Michigan State University Press, 1985), 12–42.

8. Desmond Rochfort, *Mexican Muralists* (San Francisco: Chronicle Books, 1998), 129.

9. Diego Rivera with Gladys March, *Diego Rivera: My Art, My Life* (New York: Dover, 1991), 119.

10. Downs, *The Detroit Industry Murals*, 177.

11. Bertram D. Wolfe, *The Fabulous Life of Diego Rivera* (New York: Cooper Square, 1963), 321.

12. Ibid., 325.

13. Ibid., 326.

14. Ibid., 330.

15. *New York World-Telegram*, May 12, 1933.

16. Wolfe, *The Fabulous Life of Diego Rivera*, 338.

Chapter 5

AGAIN IN MEXICO (1934–1941)

During the late 1930s and early 1940s, Diego Rivera confronted much loss in his personal and professional life. The Communist Party, which he had strongly supported, rejected him in 1929 from its membership with the accusation that he was a counterrevolutionary artist and he was flirting with Mexican and American capitalists. His health began to deteriorate from lack of nutrition, a bad kidney, and an eye infection. But much more challenging was his divorce from Frida Kahlo, which proved to take the greatest toll on Rivera. Rivera's last year in the United States was artistically unproductive and his return to his homeland did not alleviate the anguish he was undergoing.

In a letter to Leo Eloesser, Frida Kahlo wrote that when they arrived in Mexico in December 1933, Rivera was in an unpleasant mood. The first days after their arrival were consumed with tending to his needs and cooking his favorite Mexican dishes. There were times when Kahlo would cook him a huge duck *mole* (a sauce generally made with spices, chocolate, and chilies) in order to indulge his senses. When food would not lift Rivera's spirits, antique vendors would come and show him pre-Columbian figurines and this would instantly make Rivera happy again. It would take much consoling and pampering for Rivera to integrate back into the Mexican lifestyle and a creative routine.

Rivera had returned to Mexico with great disappointment over the destruction of the mural he had painted in the RCA building in Rockefeller Center. Rivera spent several months in Mexico without producing artwork until he signed a contract with the Palace of Fine Arts in Mexico City to re-create the mural that had been destroyed in New York. In November 1934, Rivera began to reconstruct his controversial work using photographs of the original *Man at the Crossroads* taken by his assistant, Lucienne Bloch.

The mural at the Palace of Fine Arts was an exact replica of the original except for a few small changes. The first change was the name of the mural, which now became known as *Man, Controller of the Universe*. In line with this new title, the image of the empowered worker was aligned with the supporting mast of the cylindrical telescope. This re-accommodation gave the composition an effect of more balance and stability. Another change Rivera made was to include the image of John D. Rockefeller Jr., who appears in a nightclub scene near a dish of syphilis bacterium magnified under a microscope. Rivera's revengeful intent was to juxtapose the images of Rockefeller and syphilis disease to represent them as synonymous.

Rivera finished the mural at the Palace of Fine Arts in 1935. It took Rivera a full year to complete the new mural because of several unforeseen complications. First of all, the original image was intended for a much larger wall, but because of the space limitations, Rivera had to adjust the mural to fit the new location. Secondly, the small payment which he received from the commission did not allow him to hire many assistants, consequently prolonging the painting process. During the year he worked on the *Man, Controller of the Universe* mural, Rivera began to have health complications that prevented him from working for extended periods. Despite such obstacles, Rivera was determined to reconstruct the mural and did not allow any difficulty to prevent him from completing it the second time.

About this time, 1935, Bertram Wolfe collaborated with Rivera on the book, *Portrait of America*, a critical commentary on the Great Depression, the Rockefeller affair, and the general social and political situation of the United States at the time.

Man at the Crossroads. *Palace of Fine Arts. Mexico City, 1934. (Photo by Manuel Aguilar-Moreno)*

After completing the mural at the Palace of Fine Arts, he painted a series of easel paintings depicting images of the working class in Mexico. Rivera emphasized the hardships of the working class, but also painted scenes of their leisure and family life, when they were not working. Scenes of dancing, of mothers and children, and of fieldworkers were common images Rivera painted during the mid-1930s. Even when he painted scenes of working-class hardships, Rivera had a colorful and sensual technique that allowed the image to take a beautiful and sometimes joyful theme. Paintings such as *El Vendedor de Flores* (1935) and *Zandunga: Baile de Tehuantepec* (1935) provided unique insight into working-class life in Mexico. A few years later, he painted a series of images of common rituals and traditions in Mexico. Paintings of these two themes are some of the most popular Rivera works in the United States.

While Rivera was painting images of the working class, he also painted a series of Mexican landscape images. Some of the landscape paintings are *Tecalpexco* (1937), *Roots* (1937), *Copalli* (1937), and

Symbolic Landscape (1940). In all of the landscape series he painted during the period between 1937 and 1940, Rivera used a similar color palette of blue and brown hues. The landscape images represented the topography and vegetation indigenous to Mexico, with a focus on roots, tree bark, and rocks. The rigid landscape juxtaposed with the soft sky give the landscape painting series a unique insight into Mexico's environment.

In 1935, Rivera joined the Liga de Escritores y Artistas Revolucionarios (League of Revolutionary Writers and Artists), or LEAR, a group of artists who opposed fascism and war. The founders of LEAR were Leopoldo Méndez, Juan de la Cabada, and Pablo O'Higgins, with Rivera as the advisor. The group published a periodical titled *Frente a Frente* (*Face to Face*), and was commissioned by the federal government to decorate the walls of the Mercado Abelardo L. Rodríguez. The artists (O'Higgins, Ramón Alva Guadarrama, Antonio Pujol, Pedro Rendón, Miguel Tzab Trejo, Angel Bracho, and Grace and Marion Greenwood) painted the mural in the market's main building located in the center of the city. Artist Isamu Noguchi was given a grant by the Guggenheim Foundation to paint the relief mural in polychrome cement and carved brick. In January 1936, LEAR was commissioned to paint the main stairway of the Sindicato de los Talleres Gráfícos de la Nación (Union of Graphic Workers of the Nation) located in Mexico City. The theme of the mural is the union struggle and the right to protest. In 1938, LEAR was dismantled and dissolved.

In the summer of that same year, Alberto Pani, who was Rivera's friend since the European years, commissioned Rivera to paint four panels for a dining room in the Hotel Reforma, a newly constructed hotel located in downtown Mexico City. Wary after the Rockefeller incident, Rivera painted four portable panels to prevent the destruction of his work if any problems arose. The subject matter for the hotel murals was an overview of traditional Mexican festivals. In Rivera's autobiography, he states, "Of the four panels, two depicted traditional Mexican festivals: one focused on the ancient Yautepec god of war, *Huitzilopochtli*, titled *Danza de Los Huichilobos* and *The Festival of Huejotzingo* (*Agustin Lorenzo*), that depicts Lorenzo, a bandit hero. The other two panels were satirical scenes of politics and socio-economic realities of Mexico. They are: *The Dictatorship* and *Folkloric and Touristic Mexico*."

Diego Rivera and Frida Kahlo in an antifascist demonstration in Mexico City, 1936. (AP Photo)

The panel titled *Danza de Los Huichilobos* depicts *Huitzilopochtli*, the Aztec deity of war who was also the sun god that brought the Aztecs to the Valley of Mexico after a long migration. In the image depicted by Rivera, indigenous people play music and dance while modern-day Mexicans hold arms and engage in war. In the backdrop of the mural is a traditional *pulqueria* which is a place where *pulque* (pre-Columbian alcoholic beverage) was sold.

In the image titled *The Festival of Huejotzingo*, Rivera painted a large image of Agustín Lorenzo mounted on a black horse with a group of soldiers firing at him. Agustín Lorenzo was a Mexican bandit who fought against the French in Mexico and was said to have unsuccessfully attempted to kidnap the Empress Carlotta. There was also a folklorist story that spoke of a bandit named Agustín Lorenzo who would steal money from the rich and in the night regretted his actions and gave the money to those in need. Rivera used this folklore as a focus in this panel for the Hotel Reforma.

Diego Rivera painting a mural at Hotel Reforma, 1936. (AP Photo)

In the two panels depicting Mexican carnival scenes, Rivera incorporated satirical ideas to further his political and social views. In one of the panels, *Folkloric and Touristic Mexico*, he depicted present Mexican life with a blond woman in the top of the panel representing a tourist from the United States. To further his irony, he depicted Mexican men as donkeys holding bags full of money made by exploiting the Mexican working class. In the bottom of the panel there is a skeleton with the word *eternidad*, and Rivera used this metaphor of eternity to express his discontent with how tourism had changed Mexico forever.

In the second panel called *The Dictatorship*, representing a Mexican carnival scene, Rivera painted another satirical scene of Mexico's political figures. In the forefront are men in symbolic uniforms wearing masks of donkeys, dogs, and sheep. These men represent the hypocrisy of social and political institutions in Mexico. The large figure grinning is the head of a Mexican capitalist who bears the features of Hitler, Mussolini, Franklin D. Roosevelt, and Mikado. Rivera had also put other details into this panel that were removed and altered by Pani's brother, Arturo. The composite personage that is the main character of the story in this panel is Plutarco Elías Calles, a former controversial president of Mexico who persecuted the Catholic Church and led a corrupt government.

Rivera completed these murals for the hotel, but Alberto Pani was not pleased and had some images altered. Rivera became enraged and began a legal dispute. Rivera prevailed and was allowed to repaint the mural as he had originally painted it, but the mural was not allowed to be viewed by the public. Eventually, the mural at the Hotel Reforma was sold to Alberto Misrachi, a private collector and friend of Rivera, and later Misrachi sold the four panels to the Instituto Nacional de Bellas Artes.

After the Hotel Reforma scandal in 1936, Rivera realized that he would not be asked to paint murals again in Mexico for some time. The Tate Gallery show, scheduled to open in London, failed and that situation encouraged Rivera to return to his other passion, political activities. In September of the same year, he joined the International Communist League (ICL), affiliated with Trotsky Fourth International. David Alfaro Siqueiros, Rivera's muralist colleague who was a significant figure in the Mexican Communist Party, publicly attacked Rivera, saying that he was a "cynical political opportunist of limited imagination and technique."[1] At a political rally in Mexico City the two controversial artists appeared on the same platform brandishing their pistols, which they waved in the air as they yelled at each other. Then they began to shoot at the same time, aiming to the ceiling and making plaster fall, while the audience began to leave the room. This artists' fight was reported by the Mexican press as a spectacular performance of Stalinism against Trotskyism.

From 1934 to 1940, General Lázaro Cárdenas del Rio was president of Mexico. Cárdenas was a progressive official who worked to cleanse the government of corrupt bureaucrats and spread equality for the workers unions. He also ended the extensive bloodshed and capital punishment in revolutionary Mexico. One of the most important contributions President Cárdenas made to Mexico and the Mexican people was the redistribution among peasants of large plots of land once owned by individual landlords.

During this time, Europe was also going through significant political turmoil. Adolf Hitler was gaining power in Germany, Benito Mussolini was dictator of Italy, and Joseph Stalin was taking control of Russia. European dictators were met by resistance from many other leaders, such as Leon Trotsky. In Russia, Trotsky and Lenin had led the Russian people against the repressive tsarist government in the 1917 October Revolution. Trotsky was the organizer of the Red Army of the Soviet Union. When Trotsky had ideological disagreements with Stalin, Trotsky was excluded from the Communist Party and exiled from Russia. The expulsion of Trotsky from Russia increased his international popularity, but also increased the dangerous conditions that threatened his life. He lived in Turkey, France, and Norway before seeking refuge in Mexico.

In September 1936, Rivera joined Trotsky's Communist International League. In November, he received a telegram from Anita Brenner asking if Mexico could give asylum to Leon Trotsky. Rivera went to the Mexican government and asked President Cárdenas to allow Trotsky to live in Mexico. President Cárdenas gave Trotsky asylum with the condition that he would not practice any political activities while in Mexico. In December 1937, Leon and Natalia Trotsky arrived in Tampico, Mexico. The Trotskys lived in the Rivera-Kahlo home in the district of Coyoacan for almost two years, guarded by two men from the Russian revolutionary movement. They were afraid that the Stalinists would come to assassinate Trotsky.

For the first year, the Riveras and the Trotskys spent much time together. During that time, André and Jacqueline Breton also arrived in Mexico. André Breton was a French poet, writer, and theorist who founded the surrealist movement, which encouraged freedom of the mind through random juxtaposing of ideas in art, film, and writing. Breton wrote the first and second Surrealist Manifestos in 1924 and 1928, which stated that one must look for freedom in life through imagination and let go of the fear that holds one to the obsession with failure instead of the contingency of good. Breton was given the title "father of surrealism" because he created a theoretical movement that was followed by many artists, writers, and filmmakers in the 1920s and 1930s.

The Bretons, the Trotskys, and the Riveras all shared the same political, social, and artistic views. Trotsky wrote an article for the *Partisan Review* that stated his common views with Rivera's artwork. Trotsky said that if one wanted to get a visual understanding of revolutionary art, one should look at Rivera's frescoes. Breton and Trotsky also worked together on various projects and would share the same Marxist ideological views. In an article titled "Literature and Revolution," Trotsky expressed his content with new art movements like futurism, which "arose as a protest against the art of petty realists who sponged on life."[2] Trotsky felt that one should not separate art from social life. This meant that "new artists will need all the methods and processes evolved in the past, as well a few supplementary ones, in order to grasp the new life . . . and that this is not going to be artistic eclecticism, because the unity of art is created by an active world-attitude and active life-attitude."[3]

Breton sought out Frida Kahlo to join the newly developed surrealist movement, for the dreamlike stories in her artwork fit perfectly into the Surrealist Manifesto statement. These common views among the artists would help build a friendship for some time, even though Kahlo never considered herself a surrealist. She always argued that her art described her pain and it was not a dream, but a bitter reality.

All three couples spent a great deal of time together and Trotsky and Kahlo began an affair that lasted for some time. Natalia Trotsky and Rivera both discovered the affair, which resulted in a split in their friendship, as well as in the Rivera-Kahlo marriage. The Trotskys moved out of the Rivera home into another house two blocks away in the same district of Coyoacan. A few months later, Stalin signed a nonaggression treaty with Hitler, which created an unsafe environment for all Trotskyists. On May 24, 1940, a group of men dressed as policemen, including the Stalinist painter David Alfaro Siqueiros, raided Trotsky's home. The Trotskys were in bed sleeping when they heard the men storm in and they quickly hid underneath the bed. The men shot up the room including the bed, but the Trotskys escaped alive. A few months later Trotsky was murdered by Ramón Mercader, a Spanish Stalinist. He disagreed with Trotsky's views and when he got the first chance to kill the Russian revolutionary, he drove an ice pick into his skull. Trotsky was rushed to the hospital, but from the brain damage inflicted by the attack, he later died. After the murder of Trotsky, Rivera went into hiding for some time thinking that he would be next. Kahlo fell into a depression and became anxious because she had known Mercader in Paris and had allowed him to have dinner in her home.

In the summer of 1935, Rivera and Kahlo separated. It is now widely known that both Rivera and Kahlo engaged in numerous extramarital affairs, but the reason for their split at this time probably had has much to do with Kahlo's affair with Trotsky as with Kahlo's discovery that Rivera was having an affair with Kahlo's younger sister, Cristina.[4] After learning of the affair, Kahlo cut off her hair and abstained from wearing her traditional *Tehuana* clothing that Rivera loved so much and that defined her style. In a letter Kahlo wrote to Dr. Eloesser, her long-time doctor and friend, she said, "I believe that by working I will forget the sorrows and I will be able to be happier. . . . I hope my stupid neurasthenia will soon go away and my life will be more normal again—but you know it is rather difficult and I will need much willpower to manage even to be enthusiastic about painting or about doing anything. Today was Diego's saint's day and we were happy and it is to be hoped there will be many days of this kind in my life." Kahlo soon moved out of the blue house and rented an apartment in Mexico City, where she lived for the next two years.

During this time, Frida Kahlo received an invitation to exhibit in a gallery in New York City. She traveled to New York in 1938, where she was part of a collective exhibition in the Julien Levy Gallery with other artists such as Isamu Noguchi, Clare Boothe Luce, and Georgia O'Keeffe. This separation allowed Rivera and Kahlo to focus on their individual artistic projects. In 1939, Kahlo continued her travels to Paris, where she exhibited her artwork at the Exhibition *Mexique*, curated by André Breton at the Pierre Colle gallery. There, she socialized with artists like Wassily Kandinsky, Pablo Picasso, and Marcel Duchamp. While in Paris, Kahlo received a phone call from Rivera asking for a divorce. Rivera later recalled that

> I telephoned her to plead for her consent to divorce, and in my anxiety, fabricated a stupid vulgar pretext. I dreaded a long, heart-wrenching discussion so much that I impulsively seized on the quickest way to my end. It worked. Frida declared that she too

wanted an immediate divorce. My "victory" quickly changed to gall in my heart. We had been married now for thirteen years. We still loved each other. I simply wanted to be free to carry on with any woman who caught my fancy.[5]

In August 1939, Rivera began a series of drawings and paintings of the North American dancer Modelle Boss. The image he painted, titled *Dancer in Repose* (1939), depicts Boss sitting on a chair holding her hair with both hands and shows her nude, voluptuous body, accentuating her every curve. During this time, Rivera also painted an image of Paulette Goddard, a North American actress and friend who at the time was married to film actor Charlie Chaplin. These friendships gave Rivera an opportunity to practice painting the female body. But he also embarked upon an affair with Goddard, even though Chaplin and

Diego Rivera and Frida Kahlo at their studio-house in San Angel, Mexico City, 1939. (AP Photo)

Goddard had invited Rivera to their home in Los Angeles and Rivera had enjoyed talking with Chaplin about film and art.

In January 1940, Rivera participated in the exhibition titled Exposición International del Surrealismo (International Exhibition of Surrealism) in the Galería de Arte Mexicano in Mexico City. The exhibition was organized by the surrealist painter Wolfgang Paalen and Peruvian poet César Moro with the help of André Breton. Two of Rivera's paintings, *The Lady in White* (1939) and *Symbolic Landscape* (1940), were included in the exhibition. This exhibition popularized the surrealist art movement in Mexico and many artists began to find interest in this interpretation of art.

While Kahlo was in Paris, Rivera received a commission from Timothy Pflueger to contribute to an Art in Action exhibit at the Golden Gate International Exposition of the San Francisco World's Fair. In

Diego Rivera at the airport in San Francisco, California, 1940. (AP Photo)

1940, Rivera arrived at Treasure Island, where the World's Fair had taken place. In the *Pan-American Unity* mural, Rivera depicted the development and growth of the American continent. His interpretation shows the union and collaboration of the Indian cultures and the *mestizo* peoples of the South with the European peoples of the industrial North for the construction of the American civilization. In the center of the mural, Rivera depicted a colossal image with two blended figures. One half of the statue is the earth goddess Coatlicue with a human hand extended in a sign of peace, and the other half is a pressing machine. The left side of the mural with Coatlicue has scenes of the indigenous peoples of the American continent. The right side of the machine has images of modern technology including airplanes and steamboats. Underneath the colossal dual figure appears the personification of Pan-American Unity, with the images of Diego Rivera and Paulette Goddard holding hands and surrounding the symbolic Tree of Life and Love. The values of the South are represented by Frida Kahlo wearing a beautiful *Tehuana* dress. Once the mural had served its purpose for the San Francisco World's Fair, the chief architect arranged for the mural to be permanently placed in the City College of San Francisco.

Rivera remained in San Francisco for another six months, during which time he received information that Kahlo was ill. He invited her to come to San Francisco, which she did a short time later. While there, Kahlo was admitted into the hospital and later released with the recommendation that she get rest and stop drinking and smoking. Before leaving San Francisco, Rivera asked Kahlo to marry him once more. She did not agree and instead left for New York to continue her work. Several months later, Kahlo returned to San Francisco and accepted Rivera's marriage offer. On December 8, 1940, Rivera and Kahlo were married for the second time in Mexico. Once he finished painting the mural in San Francisco, Kahlo and Rivera returned to Mexico and lived together again in the blue house in Coyoacan.

The mural Rivera created for the Golden Gate International Exposition of the San Francisco World's Fair was completed with great success. *Life Magazine* called Rivera a hit of the Art in Action program. The only problem was that once the fair ended, the mural was in storage for more than twenty years. Although the mural was to be sent to the San Francisco City College, there was no room large enough to accommodate it. Timothy Pflueger planned to build a library that would include a large wall for the mural, but the plans were changed. Once Pflueger died, it seemed as if the mural would never see light. In 1961, Pflueger's brother Milton designed the Arts Auditorium in the San Francisco City College and finally placed the mural in the lobby of the building.

In December 1940, General Manuel Avila Camacho was inaugurated as president of Mexico. Some of the positive things that can be attributed to President Avila Camacho were the creation in 1943 of the Mexican Institute of Social Security, a socialized medicine system, and programs for the reduction of illiteracy. Avila Camacho also helped the working class by continuing land reform and declaring a rent freeze to aid low-income households. He not only renamed the Party of the Mexican Revolution (PRM) as the Institutional Revolutionary Party (PRI), but also created new political candidacy requirements that made it impossible for communists to run for the presidency. In 1941, Rivera petitioned the Mexican Communist Party for readmittance but was rejected.

NOTES

1. Patrick Marnham, *Dreaming with His Eyes Open: A Life of Diego Rivera* (New York: Knopf, 1998), 276.
2. Leon Trotsky, "Literature and Revolution," in *Art in Theory 1900–1990: An Anthology of Changing Ideas*, ed. Charles Harrison and Paul Wood (London: Blackwell, 1992), 427.
3. Ibid.
4. Hayden Herrera, *Frida: A Biography of Frida Kahlo* (New York: First Perennial Library, 1984), 179–92.
5. Diego Rivera with Gladys March, *My Art, My Life: An Autobiography* (New York: Dover, 1991).

Chapter 6

RIVERA AND HIS MEXICAN MURALS OF THE 1940s (1941–1949)

The international political instability of the 1940s and 1950s—of World War I and the subsequent postwar and Cold War eras—inspired the Mexican government to reinforce national unity. The country entered into a stage of institutional consolidation after the revolution and an inevitable modernization, shifting from an agrarian structure into an industrial and technological urban organization. Under the presidency of Manuel Avila-Camacho, the economic and social status of workers and of the middle class grew in Mexico. The new concern of artists was to focus on Mexico as a subject. In this context of rapid changes in society and a new nationalism, Rivera's work focused inward on the theme of the roots of Mexican identity and exaltation of the cultural and technological achievements of the pre-Columbian peoples. At the same time, Rivera represented the popular history of the country in a more nostalgic and idealistic way, which appeared as a contradiction to the dynamics and tendencies of modern society.

When Rivera returned from San Francisco in 1941, he was commissioned to paint murals for the second time in the National Palace in Mexico City, this time in the corridors around the National Palace's patio. Rivera produced 11 panels that represent diverse pre-Hispanic cultures. These show an idealized indigenous paradise with peaceful scenes of indigenous life, and from there can be seen how the diverse agricultural and productive activities evolved from culture to culture. The enormous work of research and documentation that Rivera did becomes evident in the accurate and artistic representation of the subjects. The series of panels can be read from west to east on the north wall of the building. The first two panels in the series of the mural are located on either side of a doorway. The two panels are titled *Lo Que el Mundo Debe a Mexico* (*What the World Owes Mexico*, 1942) and *La Cultura del Antiguo Mexico* (*The Culture of Ancient Mexico*, 1942).

The first two panels do not consist of images, but rather a text written in Spanish and Nahuatl. Nahuatl was one of many languages spoken in Mexico during the pre-Columbian period. Rivera presents various agricultural, botanical, and architectural contributions that Mexico shared with the world. He praises the extensive Indian herbal medicine with plants such as the *yolloxochitl* that was used for cardiac ailments. He also commends the mathematical and astronomical knowledge that produced a very precise calendar and established forecasting of eclipses and planetary conjunctions. The engineering techniques to make hydraulic works and urban plans, the architecture of solid, functional, and symbolic forms, and the painting that had character and color, were also extolled. Among the agricultural achievements of the pre-Columbian world that were exported to Europe are vegetables and fruits such as pineapples, corn, chocolate, peanuts, tomato, and avocado, to name a few.

The third panel of the mural is the largest of the 11 panels and is also located on the north wall. Rivera began this section, titled *La Gran Ciudad de Tenochtitlan* (*The Great City of Tenochtitlan*), in 1945. The theme for this panel is the ancient city of Tenochtitlan, created by the Aztec culture. Rivera depicted the Aztec people in the forefront taking part in everyday tasks. Some women were depicted blending corn with a *metate* (a stone artifact used to blend and grind corn), while others trade goods in the Tlatelolco marketplace. There appears an *auianime* (prostitute), the only women in Aztec society that were allowed to use makeup and tattooing. A variety of products are sold in the crowded market, such as basketry, textiles, ceramics, flowers, grains like corn, vegetables such as beans, squashes, and chile peppers, as well as a diversity of fruits. The city of Tenochtitlan is depicted in the backdrop including its most popular features and landscapes such as pyramids, *chinampas* (artificial islands with a rectangular shape that contain fertile land to grow crops on the low waters of lake Tetzcoco), waterways, causeways, and volcanoes.

Bernal Díaz del Castillo, a soldier in Cortés's army who participated in the Spanish Conquest, stated with great amazement:

> And when we saw all those cities and villages built in the water, and other great towns on dry land, and that straight and level causeway leading to Mexico [i.e. Tenochtitlan], we were astounded. These great towns and cues [i.e., temples] and buildings rising from the water, all made of stone, seemed like an enchanted vision from the tale of Amadis. Indeed, some of our soldiers asked whether it was not all a dream. It is not surprising therefore that I should write in this vein. It was all so wonderful that I do not know how to describe this first glimpse of things never heard of, seen or dreamed of before. . . .
>
> And when we entered the city of Iztapalapa, the sight of the palaces in which they lodged us! They were very spacious and well built, of magnificent stone, cedar wood, and the wood of other sweet-smelling trees, with great rooms and courts, which were a wonderful sight, and all covered with awnings of woven cotton.
>
> When we had taken a good look at all this, we went to the orchard and garden, which was a marvelous place both to see and walk in. I was never tired of noticing the diversity of trees and the various scents given off by each, and the paths choked with roses and other flowers, and the many local fruit-trees and rose-bushes, and the pond of fresh water. Then there were birds of many breeds and varieties which came to the pond. I say again that I stood looking at it, and thought that no land like it would ever be discovered in the whole world. . . . But today all that I then saw is overthrown and destroyed; nothing is left standing.[1]

The images that appear in Rivera's mural are so accurately portrayed that they have been often utilized to illustrate anthropological books and artifacts found and sold in Mexico and the United States during the 1940s and up to the present time. Rivera began to collect Mexican pre-Columbian antiquities during this time and usually used his treasures to guide his paintings. He became a respected expert in Aztec culture and art, and this is attested to by the very accurate and realistic representations of this culture that appear throughout his murals.

The fourth, fifth, sixth, and eighth panels are depictions of specific indigenous cultures in Mexico and were all completed in 1942. The fourth panel is titled *La Civilización Tarasca* (*The Tarascan Civilization*), in which Rivera depicted the indigenous people of the state of Michoacan. There are some Indians doing agricultural activities with the circular pyramids of Tzintzuntzan and Lake Páztcuaro in the background. Some of the images in the panel were representations of industries of the Tarascan civilization, such as textile production and dyeing. Rivera also portrayed people making codices (historical-mythical pictographic books). Several codices like the *Relación de Michoacan* and *Códice Cutzio* were produced by the Tarascan people and have been extensively studied by scholars. Also included is a depiction of the metallurgy and construction industries. Remembering that Rivera was a man of great intellectual curiosity, it is no surprise that he included all these cultural elements in his murals.

In the fifth image, titled *La Civilización Zapoteca-Mixteca* (*The Zapotec-Mixtec Civilization*), Rivera painted images of common activities of the Zapotec and Mixtec peoples, such as making pottery and masks. The pottery was used for cooking, decoration, and trade in the Zapotec-Mixtec cultures. Masks were often made with the purpose of being used for special symbolic ceremonies like Dances of Fertility and Day of the Dead festivals.[2] These two aspects of the Zapotec-Mixtec culture were imperative to their artistic expression and spiritual connection. There are also shown the feather-work and gold jewelry industries. These were not just refined crafts, but traditional objects utilized in rituals of the Zapotec-Mixtec people. In the background appears the Tree of Apoala, the mythical place of origin of the Mixtec people.

The sixth panel, still located in the north wall, is titled *Civilización Totonaca* (*The Totonaca Civilization*) and was painted in 1950. It depicts the Totonacas of the city of El Tajín, which are a group of indigenous people from the eastern coastal and mountainous region of the Gulf of Mexico. This panel shows the famous Pyramid of the Niches that contains 365 cavities representing the days of the solar year. In the distance, in a plaza, are a group of people forming a circle and dancing or playing. This type of activity is similar to the *juegos de ronda* (games with children moving around a circle holding hands) still played in Mexico. There are also images of men participating in the traditional ritual celebrated by the Totonaca people called *The Dance of the Voladores* (*The Flyers Dance*). It consists of a tall pole with a man on top playing a drum. At the same time, four other men tied by a rope to a square piece also in the topmost part of the pole, which represents the four directions of the universe (cardinal points), descend to the ground in 13 rotations. This ritual performance represents the flight the gods make to come down to earth while having to pass the 13 levels of the celestial world.[3] In Mexico today, this ritual dance is still practiced and represents the same spiritual journey.

In the seventh panel, titled *La Producción Indigena de Caucho* (*The Indigenous Production of Rubber*), painted in 1950, Rivera chose to depict the everyday image of a man collecting rubber from the latex tree in order to express the importance of rubber in Mexico, specially for its use in the ball games and in religious rituals where rubber was burned to honor the gods. The eighth panel, titled *La Civilización Huasteca* (*The Huastec Civilization*), is similar to the previous panels at the National Palace and depicts the culture and traditions of this particular indigenous group. In the mural, Rivera paints the Huastec people planting and tending to their corn crops. The women are shown using the *metate* (mealing stone) to grind their corn, which will then be made into tortillas or *atole* (corn-based hot drink; corn gruel). In the backdrop appears *Chicomecoatl*, a fertility goddess responsible for the growth of maize, who carries ears of corn. The Huastec people still live in the states of San Luis Potosí, Tamaulipas, and the north of Veracruz, and own land that is excellent for the production of agriculture.

Similar to panel eight, the next panels represent the use of two other products in Mexico, chocolate and *amate* paper. Rivera chose to paint these two plants native to Mexico to further emphasize the biological and cultural developments of the various indigenous peoples of Mexico. The chocolate (cacao) was used to produce a water-based cold bitter beverage consumed by the noble class and priests. There were cases in which this beverage was mixed with chile peppers, hallucinogenic substances, or alcoholic infusions that produced altered states of consciousness for religious purposes. The cacao beans were also used as currency and therefore much appreciated. In the last panel, Rivera closed the series with an image titled *Desembarco de Los Españoles en Veracruz* (*The Disembarkation of the Spaniards in Veracruz*), painted in 1951. Rivera depicted the conquistadores in the forefront of the mural sharing the booty of gold, while other Spaniards are shown killing the indigenous people of Mexico. In the backdrop, Rivera painted a landscape scene with indigenous people hanging from trees while others are used as slaves.

Near the top of the left corner of the mural, Rivera illustrated a Christian cross and a monk blessing the land. Next to the monk appears Hernán Cortés, represented as an emaciated, hunchbacked, syphilitic, and degenerate man, with a sword pointed at indigenous people who are offering him a tribute of gold. This panel shows Rivera's strong defense of the Mesoamerican civilizations, and his contempt of the Spaniards' evil. It is a satirical commentary on the complicated political and social implications of the Spanish Conquest of Mexico. This caricature of Cortés was based, according to Rivera, on the scientific studies of an expert in legal medicine, Dr. Alfonso Quiroz, who determined the pathology of the case, and the archaeologist Eulalia Guzmán, who conducted the historical research. For ideological reasons these scholars constructed this grotesque portrait as the real Cortés, arguing that the history books that present him as a glorious conquistador were wrong.

The entire mural at the National Palace focused on two themes: the vitality and cultural advancement that pre-Columbian Mexico had before the arrival of the Spaniards, and the negative implications the conquest had on the indigenous people. Along the north wall, Rivera presented a total of 10 panels and 20 *grisailles* (a style of monochromatic painting in shades of gray, used especially to produce the optical illusion of relief sculpture) depicting the traditions, rituals, and daily customs of the indigenous people of Mexico. He painted the dignified history of the pre-Columbian cultures and their contributions to civilization. The narrative ends with the tragic Spanish Conquest.

In April 1943, Rivera and various other artists, writers, philosophers, and scientists were founding members of the Colegio Nacional

(National Academy of Mexico). The National Academy was a cultural society that included the most prominent intellectuals of Mexico, and was created to promote and support the arts and sciences. Ignacio Chávez, a noted cardiologist and also a founding member of the National Academy, later that same year, commissioned Rivera to paint two panels for the inauguration of the new building of the National Institute of Cardiology in Mexico City. The murals were titled *Historia de la Cardiología Antigua* and *Historia de la Cardiología Contemporánea* (*History of Ancient Cardiology* and *History of Modern Cardiology*), which presented the traditional and modern techniques of practicing medicine. The murals are organized with a semispiral composition that produces dynamism and requires the viewer to follow an ascending visual axis.

Rivera represented the adversities medicine faced in the past and the advances medicine had achieved with modernity. In the first panel, Rivera painted the danger that scientists of the past faced with their discoveries and thoughts, in particular the case of the Spanish physician, theologian, cartographer, and humanist Miguel Servet, who was the discoverer of pulmonary circulation and who was burned at the stake by the Calvinists for expressing supposedly heretical ideas. Read from the bottom to the top, the mural shows the advances that cardiology has brought to prolonging life. Images of early microscopes and drawings of hearts imply the deeper understanding of the human body developed by science. In this first panel the thematic line consist of portraits of cardiologists related to anatomy, physiology, the experimental method, pathology, methods of exploratory practice, clinicians and teachers, and microanatomists.

In the second panel, Rivera painted the progress cardiology has had in modern times with images of laboratories, medical teaching and research, and the discovery of X-rays to improve diagnosis. Portraits are presented of cardiologists as therapists, experimenters, semiologists (scientists that study signs and symbols), and clinicians. The physicians appear studying the mechanism of circulation, applying electrical energy for penetrating heart recesses, tracing of heart activity through electrical means, and dealing with congenital malformations. The mural ends with a child being cared for by a doctor and a vibrant tree that represents the growth of knowledge. In the backdrop, Rivera painted an image of the National Institute of Cardiology to further emphasize the positive effect that science and the university have on society. Chávez had commissioned Rivera to paint the complexity science had achieved in the advancement of medicine and consequently of the quality of human life.

At the bottom of both panels, Rivera painted four *grisailles* containing images of ancient medicine. At the bottom of the first panel, he depicted two sections containing ancient Chinese medicine and ancient Greek medicine. In the second panel he depicted two sections containing the use of the herbal cardiac stimulant *Strophanthin* in ancient African medicine and the use of the flower *Yolloxochitl* for cardiac afflictions in ancient Mexican medicine. The four sections at the bottom of the two panels specifically express the form of cardiology practiced during ancient times. The mural at the National Institute of Cardiology is a pictorial document of the efforts made by many scientists that contributed to modern heart medicine.[4]

Also in this year of 1943, both Diego Rivera and Frida Kahlo were invited to teach at the recently created art school, La Esmeralda. The academy boasted 22 professors with artistic talent who had a nationalist orientation. This was an opportunity for Rivera to have an influence on the formation of Mexican artists. Besides the formal classes in the school, Rivera took his students to paint in the streets of diverse cities and in the countryside, with the purpose of getting inspiration directly from Mexican life and landscapes. From this period of 1943 to 1945 came his watercolor series, *The Eruption of Volcano Paricutín*, and his oil painting, *Day of the Dead*.[5] In this same year, Rivera was commissioned to paint a series of panels for the new Ciro's nightclub in the Hotel Reforma. The theme for this cycle of panels was a playful representation of nude pin-up girls. For this work, Rivera did not use professional models, but volunteers.[6]

In 1941, Frida Kahlo had acquired a large plot of land on the lava bed of the Pedregal area that had been formed as a result of the eruption in ancient times of the volcano Xitle. Rivera wanted to build there a structure he had dreamed about for a long time.[7] From 1943 until his death in 1957, Rivera worked on constructing a building planned to be his home, studio, museum, and tomb. With the help of Kahlo, his daughter Ruth, and advisory from architects Frank Lloyd Wright and Juan O'Gorman, Rivera designed the *Anahuacalli*, a building that resembles a Mesoamerican pyramid and was constructed out of volcanic material indigenous to the area. The word *Anahuacalli* can be translated loosely from the Nahuatl language as "The House of all Mexicans." The building was designed to house the 60,000-plus pre-Columbian antiquities that Rivera had acquired since returning to Mexico from Europe in 1910. Rivera's purpose for creating the structure was to present to the Mexican people this collection of what he had rescued of their heritage. This was a modern ruin, the first pyramid built in Mexico in more than 500 years.

Rivera designed the structure to embody an eclectic mix of Aztec, Maya, and traditional styles with his own artistic contribution. The exterior walls of the structure were created out of irregularly cut lava rocks and the interior of the structure was constructed to have three levels. The first floor consists of a labyrinth of galleries with niches along the walls to store his artifacts and idols. The doorways have the shape of Mayan false arches and the ceilings are decorated with mosaics of pre-Columbian inspiration designed by Rivera. The sculptural motifs were also designed by the artist, and consist of snakes, jaguars, masks, and diverse elements of Mesoamerican lineage.

The second floor was designed for Rivera's personal art studio. Although Rivera did not live to see the art studio completed, it was designed to have wide terraces and large windows that would allow the view of the lava-flow from the distant volcanoes. The third and upper floor is composed of several rooms, and from the roof is visible the magnificent sea of lava with outgrowths of cactus, scrubs, and moss. On a clear day, the volcanoes Popocatepetl and Iztaccihuatl can be seen in the backdrop. Rivera also designed various halls and rooms dedicated to specific gods and goddesses that are also represented in mosaic murals on the walls and ceilings. Some of those rooms and halls were named, such as the Chamber of the Rain God, Tlaloc, which includes a stairway designed to represent the *Cenote Sagrado*, or sacred well of the Maya. Other rooms include the Nuptial Chamber, Hall of the Kings, Hall of the Sacred Temazcal, Hall of the Purifying Bath, and so on. The goddess of night is located in a small room almost completely dark. The ceilings are decorated with abstract images of pre-Conquest art in brightly colored mosaics. One of them represents a serpent that is emitting from her mouth a series of hieroglyphs that correspond to a toad, the affectionate nickname that Kahlo gave to Rivera. Although Rivera thoughtfully planned all of the details, most of the decor was executed well after his death.

Rivera's *Anahuacalli* was under construction throughout World War II and was used as a place of retreat by Rivera and Kahlo. After the war, it was converted to a museum for Rivera's collections. He ultimately spent more than $100,000 in planning and building the structure, and it is estimated that he spent another $100,000 on the collection of archaeological pieces housed there. Aside from the cost of the collection and the actual construction of *Anahuacalli*, Rivera also paid a weekly fee of $125 for maintaining the museum, exhausting his funds and leaving him with very little money remaining for living expenses.[8]

In that postwar period, and coinciding with Rivera's construction of the *Anahuacalli*, Miguel Alemán became president of Mexico from 1946 to 1952. In his earlier years, Alemán was a successful attorney representing miners suffering from silicosis and defending workers against corporations. He won many cases obtaining indemnities and compensations for miners and workers injured at work and gained favor with Mexico's labor unions. He was the first civilian president since the Mexican Revolution representing the Institutional Revolutionary Party (PRI). His administration was characterized by solid industrial development, an increase of the extension of the nation's rail network, improvement of highways, construction of a number of major schools, efficient irrigation and farming systems, development of a tourism infrastructure (in particular the beach resort of Acapulco), and a general growth of the economy. He negotiated a major loan with the United States and was the first Mexican president to visit the United States. Alemán developed a peaceful and prudent diplomatic foreign policy, and worked with the United States on the agreement and coordination of the *bracero* program (guest worker program) that lasted from 1942 to 1964. At the same time, there developed a rampant political corruption and cronyist capitalism that would shape the relationship of politics and big business in Mexico until the present day. Despite these drawbacks, President Alemán strongly influenced the development of social and economic programs to elevate the quality of life of the people of Mexico, and he finished his presidential term as one of the richest men in the world.[9]

During this period of the 1940s, Rivera had sexual affairs with several beautiful women, such as Linda Christian, the poet Pita Amor, and the actresses Paulette Goddard, Dolores del Rio, and María Félix. In 1949, he informed Kahlo, to whom he was still married, that he was intending to marry Félix. The legendary María Félix was one of the stars of the Golden Age of the Mexican Cinema between 1940 and 1955, and had a reputation as a *devoradora de hombres* (man-eating woman). Rivera's tumultuous sexual life was always the subject of commentaries by the Mexican press and the general public. He said in one occasion that "he loved women so much that he sometimes thought he must be a Lesbian."[10] Kahlo's sexuality was also speculated upon and serious rumors of the time stated that Pita Amor, Dolores del Río, and María Félix were also lovers of Frida Kahlo.[11] In 1946, Rivera had found a new art dealer to represent him by the name of Emma Hurtado, whom he would marry after Kahlo's death. Hurtado gained the exclusive rights to sell Rivera's work in her gallery, named Galería Diego Rivera.

Also in 1946, Rivera was commissioned to paint a mural in the main dining room of the new Hotel del Prado. A short time later, Rivera got pneumonia and was admitted into the American-British Hospital in Mexico City. While in the hospital, he worked on a sketch for the Hotel del Prado mural titled *Sueño de Una Tarde de Domingo en La Alameda* (*Dream of a Sunday Afternoon in the Alameda*). The theme of the mural is a combination of his childhood experiences and memories in the park as well as public figures associated with the history of Mexico. The story line was set in the *Porfiriato* period and depicts the social prejudices that were prevalent during this period in Mexican history.

Rivera began painting the complex and dense mural in 1947. He used soft and bright colors that make the composition very joyful. At the center of the mural, Diego Rivera painted himself as a young boy. He appears holding hands with a skeleton, the famous character *Calavera Catrina* (*The Elegant Skeleton*), who in turn holds the hand of the renowned engraver José Guadalupe Posada. In this way, Rivera portrays himself as a grandson of the *Calavera* and Posada, whom Rivera considered his childhood mentor and who had, in fact, created the *Calavera Catrina*. In this way, Rivera represents the influence of this national icon upon his own identity as an artist, his identification with Posada's

Detail of mural A Dream of a Sunday Afternoon in Alameda Park. *Mexico City, 1947–1948. (Photo by Manuel Aguilar Moreno)*

seminal and nationalistic art. The *Calavera Catrina* symbolizes Mexico with its *mestizo* identity that was the result of several centuries of a transculturation process in which the indigenous and the Spanish peoples integrated. This duality is expressed with the contrast between the European dress and hat of the *Calavera* on one side, and on the other side, the buckle with the symbol *Ollin*, the Aztec concept of movement, and her stole that is the feather serpent, the god Quetzalcoatl, a symbol of fertility in the Indian world.

Standing behind the child Diego in the painting is the figure of Frida Kahlo, who appears as his mother and bears in her left hand the symbol of yin-yang, which in the Asian and pre-Columbian cultures represents the duality of the forces of life and the universe. Around this group, in the foreground, are scenes representing the outcasts and poor people living during the dictatorship of Porfirio Díaz, such as Mexican Indian peasants, pickpockets, street and newspaper vendors, homeless people, and, with a yellow dress, the defiant prostitute Lupe, *la revoltosa*, the rebellious woman. These are the underdogs, on whose behalf the revolution was made. They contrast with the well-dressed figures representing Mexico's ruling class including the dictator Porfirio Díaz and his wife Carmen. Surrounding this central group are the poet Manuel Gutiérrez Nájera, the father of the first Cuban revolution, José Martí, and General "Lobo" Guerrero, a highly decorated hero of the war against the French, also known as General Medals.

The history depicted in the mural appears as told and witnessed by the Alameda Park itself. On the left part of the fresco, there is a group of colonial and 19th-century personages with a dramatic image of an individual being burned at the stake by the Spanish Inquisition (which had its burning grounds in the park). Next are, among others, the figures of the conquistador Hernán Cortés, the Viceroy Luis de Velasco, the first bishop of Mexico, Juan de Zumárraga, the great feminist poet Sor Juana Inés de la Cruz, the emperor Maximilian and his wife Carlota who came during the French Intervention, the infamous President Antonio López de Santa Ana, and General Winfield Scott, the commander of the United States Army that invaded Mexico, and whose troops camped in the Alameda in 1847. As a consequence of this flagrant invasion, Mexico lost half of its territory, an area that now consists of the states of California, Nevada, Arizona, Utah, Colorado, New Mexico, Texas, and part of Wyoming.

On the right-hand part of the mural is a crowd of people representing the violent revolution of 1910 against the oppression of colonialism and tyranny. Among them can be seen Francisco Madero, the instigator of the movement, Emiliano Zapata, the great agrarian leader, and generals Victoriano Huerta and Manuel Mondragón, who played an obscure role in the conflict. Near the revolutionary scene are Rivera's second wife Lupe Marín with her two daughters, Ruth and Lupe. The colorful composition has a theatrical and nostalgic atmosphere. This Alameda mural is a unique masterpiece that intertwines autobiography, history, and fantasy. It is a narrative of the popular history of Mexico.

Although the Alameda mural does not contain any direct socialist or explicit political contents like many of Rivera's earlier works, it was not exempt from controversy. On the left side, among the group of 19th-century liberal politicians affiliated with the republican government of President Benito Juárez, Rivera depicted the radical philosopher Ignacio Ramírez, also known as the Nigromante (the black magician), who, during a lecture at the Letrán Academy in Mexico City in 1836, uttered the words "God does not exist," which was considered offensive and blasphemous by the Catholic Church. As Rivera painted the Nigromante holding a placard with the offensive inscription, it incurred a strong public protest and Mexico City's archbishop Luis Martínez refused to bless the newly built hotel in which the mural had been painted. A group of outraged Catholic students physically attacked the mural, damaging the face of the figure of the young Rivera and scratching out the offending words on the placard. Rivera restored the fresco, but as he did not want to remove the Ramírez statement, it was covered from the public view for eight years.[12] Finally in 1956, Rivera, who his entire life had presented himself as an atheist and communist, in a sudden, surprising, and contradictory statement, declared that he was a Catholic. He said that he did not have the intention of offending the Catholic people of Mexico and replaced the atheist words in the placard with an inscription that stated: "Academia de Letrán 1836," a reference merely to the site where the Nigromante gave the controversial speech. After this action, the infamous and beautiful mural of the Alameda Park was unveiled and shown in full to the public.

In 1985 a strong earthquake in Mexico City destroyed and damaged several buildings in the downtown area. The Hotel del Prado was badly damaged and needed to be demolished. In a spectacular and daring action, the government rescued the celebrated mural and moved it to a new location on the opposite side of Alameda Park where a special building, the Museo Mural Diego Rivera, was built to lodge it.

In 1949, the Mexican government, through the National Institute of Fine Arts, organized a magnificent retrospective exhibit to celebrate 50 years of Rivera's career. The impressive exhibit presented more than a thousand of his works, and was inaugurated by President Miguel Alemán in the Palace of Fine Arts of Mexico City. The exhibition was a tremendous success and was accompanied by the publication of a beautiful and comprehensive monograph-catalogue named *Diego Rivera: 50 Years of Artistic Work*. With their enthusiastic response to the exhibit, the Mexican people showed their great respect for and recognition of the controversial artist.

NOTES

1. Bernal Díaz del Castillo, *The True History of the Conquest of Mexico* (New York: McBride, 1938).

2. N.C. Christopher Couch, *Faces of Eternity: Masks of the Pre-Columbian Americas* (New York: Americas Society, 1991).

3. Patricia Petersen, *Voladores* (Columbus, OH: Peter Bedrick Books, 2002).

4. Cynthia Newman Helms, *Diego Rivera: A Retrospective* (New York: Founders Society Detroit Institute of Arts, in association with Norton, 1986), 221–315.

5. Andrea Kettenman, *Rivera* (Köln: Taschen, 1997), 72–73.

6. Diego Rivera with Gladys March, *My Art, My Life: An Autobiography* (New York: Dover, 1991), 154.

7. Bertram D. Wolfe, *The Fabulous Life of Diego Rivera* (New York: Cooper Square Press, 2000), 370.

8. Ibid., 370–73.

9. María Antonia Martínez, *El despegue constructivo de la Revolución: Sociedad y Política* (Mexico: Ciesas-Porrúa, 2004).

10. Patrick Marnham, *Dreaming with His Eyes Open: A Life of Diego Rivera* (Berkeley: University of California Press, 1998), 306–9.

11. Ibid.

12. Desmond Rochfort, *Mexican Muralists* (San Francisco: Chronicle Books, 1998), 173–75.

Chapter 7

THE FINAL YEARS (1950–1957)

Rivera spent most of 1950 by Frida Kahlo's side in the hospital while she recovered from her spine operation. He took a small room next to his wife and slept every night in the hospital with the exception of Tuesdays, which he set aside for working at *Anahuacalli*. He saw Kahlo suffer terrible pain from the many back surgeries she had and the gangrene she developed on her toes. Although Kahlo experienced intense physical pain throughout her life, she continued to paint, with Rivera's encouragement.

While tending to Kahlo in the hospital and working on the *Anahuacalli*, he was asked to illustrate the cover for Pablo Neruda's book titled *Canto General*. The book was a compilation of poems written by Neruda, covering a range of topics such as creation and the Americas. Rivera also worked in collaboration with David Alfaro Siqueiros, a Mexican painter and muralist during that period. The illustration, titled *Pre-Hispanic America*, depicts various scenes of the Aztec and Peruvian cultures. It is divided in two, with the left side representing the Aztec culture and the right side depicting the Peruvian culture. In the center, there is a sacrificed man on top of a pyramid with the sun hovering over the scene. The sacrificed man gives his life as an offering to the sun god and that allows the sun to come out and produce day and therefore life. To the left, there is another pyramid with an image of the death god, Mictlantecuhtli. Underneath this pyramid there is another sacrificial scene and a group of Aztecs involved in agricultural as well as arts and crafts activities. To the right of these scenes appears a woman cooking and a man making a pot. Underneath the Aztec side of the image, there are serpents and shells depicted near a flow of water, illustrating the idea of fertility.

On the right side of the painting, titled *Pre-Columbian America,* there are images depicting the Peruvian culture. In the center, there is an image of the construction of Machu Picchu by the Inca culture. Above the mountains are images of wildlife including the condor of the Andes, which is indigenous to that area. On the lower part of the image there is a woman spinning yarn, making textiles, which are common in Peru. To the right there is another woman with a *metate* preparing food. Beneath the entire scene are more shells that reinforce the symbolic idea of fertility and creation of man and animals.

After finishing the illustration with Siqueiros, Rivera exhibited his artwork in the Mexican pavilion at the Venice Biennale. He exhibited along with artists such as Clemente Orozco and Rufino Tamayo. Rivera also designed the scenery for the play titled *The Quadrant of Solitude* by José Revueltas. The play opened in May 1950 at the Arbeu Theatre in Mexico City. Rivera worked diligently in his art throughout the year, but toward the end he began to campaign for the Stockholm Peace Conference, an event that had the purpose of stopping the production of nuclear bombs.

In 1951, Rivera was commissioned to paint an impressive hydraulic works project that consisted in decorating the sides and bottom of the Lerma River water collection building. The Lerma River is Mexico's second largest river, which begins in Mexico City and ends in Lake Chapala, located in the state of Jalisco. Rivera was asked to paint the interior of the water collecting tank, located in a small building in the second section of the Chapultepec Park in Mexico City. There, the water was purified and distributed to diverse parts of the city. This was to be his first (and only) mural partially submerged under water. Rivera understood that accepting this task meant exploring new materials that would have to withstand the water in the reservoir. Although Rivera studied various substances in order to create a long-lasting mural, he failed to understand the force water had over a long period of time. In consequence the mural eventually suffered damages in its surface and a gradual color fading.

In February of that year, Rivera began to paint this mural. Titled *Water: Origin of Life*, it incorporated the function and structure of the Lerma River reservoir to further explore his evolutionary theme. The mural's subject represented the importance water had for the evolution of all life forms. He began his mural at the mouth of the reservoir, the location where a large drainpipe opened and released the flow of water. Above the opening of the pipe, Rivera painted two large hands cupping water that was overflowing through the fingers and onto the bottom of the reservoir. At the floor of the reservoir runs a river in which Rivera painted various forms of protoplasmic life. He used stylized lines and curves to represent the water as well as to add movement and symmetry to the protoplasmic organisms that fill the reservoir floor.

On the walls of the reservoir, Rivera painted a man and a woman emerging from an embryo surrounded by the protoplasmic organisms that create life. Rivera continued to paint the evolution of life by incorporating man's transmutation. An image of a monkey is depicted holding the hand of a man representing Darwin's evolutionary theory. This metamorphosis is not only depicted in man's creation but also in the creation of animals such as the tadpole, which transforms into a frog. Throughout the entire mural, Rivera also infuses science and agricultural themes to further explain the role that nature and science have in the world. The history of the construction of the aqueduct was also depicted in the mural. Rivera included scenes of man's creation to blend the function of the site with the space.

Outside of the water collector building, he created a huge relief sculpture of *Tlaloc*, the Aztec water god. The image of the god was made with a mosaic of stones and is submerged in a shallow pool of water, forming a unique type of fountain. The sculpture that symbolizes the water as a vital element for human life becomes even more spectacular when seen from the sky. In this monumental work, Rivera achieved plastic integration, which is the use of painting, sculpture, and architecture interacting together and forming a unit.

Once Rivera finished the Lerma River mural he began to give a series of lectures at the Colegio Nacional (Academy of Arts and Sciences) on the subject of art and politics. The lectures gave Rivera an opportunity to speak publicly about his murals and their direct correlation with his political ideas. Rivera and Kahlo continued to socialize in Mexico's artistic circles with people such as photographer Bernice Kalko, artist Dolores del Rio, and poet Carlos Pellicer, several of whom proved to be loyal friends through the end of their lives.

In 1952, Rivera was commissioned to paint a portable mural titled *The Nightmare of War and the Dream of Peace* for an exhibition of Mexican art that was going to travel to Europe and was organized by Carlos Chávez, the director of the Fine Arts Institute. Rivera sketched a preliminary draft that was reviewed by Chávez and accepted. When Rivera was close to finishing the mural, he received information that his image would have to be reviewed by the Minister of Education based on some of the content in the painting. A few days later, Rivera was denied participation in the exhibition. The images of Stalin and Mao Tse-tung offering a pen and peace treaty to the symbols of capitalism, such as John Bull, Uncle Sam, and Belle Marianne (an image of a woman with a Phrygian cap that personified an allegory of freedom and republic in the French Revolution), were considered offensive and provocative by the exhibition organizers. Rivera had signed a contract allowing him to place it in the Fine Arts Palace after the exhibition, and he did so. A few days later, Rivera's mural was stolen from the Fine Arts Palace, and according to Chávez's story, the mural was taken by 15 masked man during the night.

Soon after this occurrence, Rivera and the chief of the administrative department of the Fine Arts Institute, Miss Leonor Llach, went to the attorney general's office to file a report on the missing painting. According to Rivera, Miss Llach changed Chávez's story and told the truth, that the painting was cut out of the frame and stored in the palace. Rivera immediately phoned the press about these happenings and instigated a public scandal. Two hours later, Rivera's attorney received a phone call from Chávez asking Rivera to withdraw his statement to the press in return for his stolen painting and other materials used to paint the mural. Rivera agreed and received his painting, which was subsequently acquired by the Chinese government; to this day, its precise location remains unknown.

That same year of 1952, Rivera began to research and sketch images for a mosaic relief mural he was asked to create for the stadium at the Universidad Nacional de Mexico (UNAM). The theme of this mural was *sports in Mexican history* from the pre-Columbian period to the present. Rivera began to work on the mural in May, but hindered by lack of money only managed to complete the front section of the stadium of the UNAM, which would later be used for the Olympic Games of 1968.

In 1953, Rivera was asked to decorate the façade of the Teatro de Los Insurgentes. The structure was built on one of the busiest streets in Mexico City called Avenida de los Insurgentes and functioned as a motion picture theater. The owner, José María Dávila, and the architect of the building, Alejandro Prieto, asked Rivera to decorate the façade above the marquee. The space measured approximately 150 feet long and approximately 32 feet high. With a staff of 17 assistants working 12 hours a day, Rivera began his new work. His first radical decision was to use glass mosaic tiles to decorate the façade. He chose to use mosaic as his medium because he wanted to call attention to his work, which would otherwise be lost in the fast-paced life of a large city like Mexico City. In strategically choosing mosaic as his material, he was able to reflect a shimmer that would catch the attention of people walking, flying, or driving by.

Rivera's mosaic mural is titled *A History of Theater in Mexico* and portrays the social and historical events that theater often captures. As these events are often presented in theater with raw expression, Rivera felt able to explore his social views using important Mexican iconic figures. Personages like Miguel Hidalgo, Hernán Cortés, and Cantiflas were incorporated into his mosaic mural to weave together the story of theater and culture in Mexico's history.

Above the center of the marquee, Rivera portrayed a mask, the traditional symbol of theater, being put in place by the elegantly decorated hands of a woman. The mask contains a sun and moon in the center of the forehead, symbolizing the Aztec idea of regeneration (death and life). The sun (day) and moon (night) together represent the balance and duality needed to continue life's cycle. Above the mask is a scene of a comedic Mexican actor named Cantinflas, famous for his deep social commentary directed at the Mexican culture. In this particular depiction, Cantiflas was portrayed at the center of the scene dressed in run-down clothing with his hands extended with two stars above his head and Mexico City's landscape in the background. On one side of Cantinflas there is a group of wealthy people dressed in extravagant clothing. Rivera portrayed the Catholic Church in this group of people, expressing in this way his views toward the excesses of the church. With his extended hand, Cantiflas is taking money from the rich and giving it to the poor located on the other side. The underprivileged, who consist of children, the elderly, and the handicapped, appear with their hands extended, asking for money. Underneath the rich are stacks of gold that create the platform from which they stand and the platform for the poor consists of a scale that is at zero.

To the left of the center depiction of Cantinflas, there is a scene that depicts Hernán Cortés stabbing a Mexican Indian in the back with a sword. The indigenous person is on his knees with his hands tied behind his back as a speech scroll symbolizing sound comes out of his mouth. Under the indigenous man is a bed of corn that represents the main food that gives sustenance to the Mexican people. Above this scene is a couple that symbolizes the Spanish culture and its looting of Mexican richness. To the right of the Spanish woman is a man that seems to be the viceroy dressed in elegant attire, holding a stick that is in motion to strike the indigenous man, who is kneeling on the ground. On the left side of this scene, there is an archangel with a grotesque face who wears armor and is holding a dagger. He is looking down with complacence at Cortes, who stands on a pile of gold coins. Above the entire scene is a monumental devil with horns looking onto the scene.

Just to the right of Rivera's critique of Spanish rule in Mexico, the images of Miguel Hidalgo, José María Morelos, and Benito Juárez are depicted as Mexican figures who represent liberty and independence. These heroic figures are facing three scenes of postcolonial effects within Mexico. In the first scene are two *charros* playing music and singing with a woman who is seated on the ground. On top of this scene there is a woman crying, the Empress Carlota, who became mentally ill as a consequence of the killing of her husband Emperor Maximilian of Habsburg by order of President Juárez in defense of the Mexican Republic. Above is an image of a fist, symbolizing strength.

To the right of the mural are scenes of the indigenous people of Mexico performing diverse rituals. Images of Aztec gods and ceremonial acts such as a human sacrifice appear to express the divine value of the creation of man and the philosophical thought about life and death for the Mexican indigenous cultures. Images of Emiliano Zapata and the revolution of 1910 were all depicted to further narrate the Mexican experience into modernity. Thus, the diverse representations in a theatrical style of the pre-Columbian cultures, the Spanish Conquest, and the Independent period in this mural present a didactic commentary on the history of Mexico and its significant individuals.

Like many of Rivera's previous murals, he received criticism for some controversial scenes. His criticism and satire on the Catholic Church depicted in the mural disturbed some of the community. Rivera's portrayal of a priest on the side of the rich, symbolically represented with a gesture of greed, offended some religious people. In addition, some sectors of the society reacted when Cantinflas appeared with a medallion of the Virgin of Guadalupe, involving her in the dispute between rich and poor, which was considered a mockery. At the same time it seemed as if the church was seeing the image of Cantinflas as holy or saint-like. Rivera felt forced to erase the depiction of the Virgin in the scene in response to the controversy, but stated, "Cantinflas is an artist who symbolizes the people of Mexico, and the *Virgen de Guadalupe* is the banner of their faith."[1] In sum, this mural combined popular Mexican ideas with Rivera's critical and analytical views.

In 1953, Rivera was commissioned to paint yet another public mural for La Raza Hospital in Mexico City. The mural was painted on double movable panels, a method that Rivera had developed. His technique consisted of using composition board, which was attached to a large wood panel. He then spread a material consisting of goat's hair, marble dust, and lime across the panel, and before it dried Rivera laid wire mesh grid over the entire surface and allowed it to set before he put plaster on top of it. Once the plaster was dry, he applied another thin coat and would paint on it, permitting the paint to dry into the plaster. This process allowed the paint to embed into the plaster and therefore into the wall.

For the mural titled *The History of Medicine*, Rivera thoroughly researched ancient and modern medical practices in Mexico and accurately presented a timeline of medical discoveries. In the center of the panel, Rivera painted a large image of *Tlazolteotl* or *Ixcuina*, the Aztec goddess of purification, healing, and childbirth, to which confessions were said to in order to cleanse oneself from sin.[2] Rivera used the Codex Borbonicus to directly get the image of the goddess in her complete authentic depiction. In the codex image and the mural, the goddess is represented squatting in the act of giving birth to a child. The goddess *Tlazolteotl* was also considered to have different personas, including *Teteoinnan*, the mother of all the gods who was worshiped with great devotion by the people. As one scholar explains,

> Her devotees were physicians, leeches, those who cured sickness of the intestine, those who purged people, and eye doctors. Also women, midwives, those who brought about abortions, who read the future, who cast auguries by looking upon water or by casting grains of corn, who read fortunes by use of knotted cords, who cured sickness by removing stones or obsidian knives from the body, who removed worms from the teeth, who removed worms from the eyes.[3]

In Rivera's profound understanding of *Tlazolteotl* and her various facets, he rightfully chose this goddess as a symbol for medicine at La Raza Hospital.

Below *Tlazolteotl*, Rivera depicted 84 tiles with images of medicinal plants and their *Nahuatl* names painted on them. At the bottom of the unfinished table of tiles, there is a woman kneeling as she paints the plants onto the tablets. Rivera researched the medicinal plants from the Codex de La Cruz-Badiano in order to accurately depict their authentic botanical features. Underneath the table, there are two serpents facing each other. The serpents are growing out of two trees, one red and the other yellow, which flank both sides of the panels. In between the two serpents Rivera depicted a mask with half of its face in skeletal form and the other with flesh. In pre-Columbian times, the mask was a common object used to conduct funerary ceremonies. Rivera used the mask and trees to represent the duality of life and death, as many ancient cultures had done in the past.

On the right side of the panel, there are scenes depicting the history of medicine in ancient Mexico. Images of childbirth, surgery, and how ancient indigenous medicine men cured people are depicted in this side of the mural. There are eight Aztec physicians depicted in the mural and they are portrayed "carrying on their backs a paper mitre-shaped cap, which have a protruding spindle, cotton flowers, and quetzal feathers."[4] These men had the important task of carrying out surgeries and giving medicine to the ill. Rivera also depicted a priest dressed in the costume of *Tlazolteotl* who appears aiding in healing the sick. Rivera included this image to further exemplify the significance of the goddess and her attributes. In the lower right corner of the pre-Columbian side of the panel, there is an image of *Tlazolteotl* perched on a swing from a tree branch. Rivera's image of the goddess is a replica of an Aztec sculpture from about1500. This image represents the goddess squatting with her knees spread, giving birth to a human being. Rivera further explored the fertility notion by illustrating the branch to personify a penis. Spiraling over the pre-Columbian side of the mural is a sun representing the movement and transcendence of life.

On the left side of the mural, Rivera portrayed modern science and medicine. Images of X-ray machines, the discovery of blood transplants, and modern surgical procedures are depicted in the modern side of the mural. Above the scene of modern science, he painted a moon to balance the spinning sun on the opposite side. The moon, which represents night, femaleness, and death, did not necessarily have a negative connotation, but rather represented the need for balance in every aspect of human life. Rivera used man's medical discoveries in pre-Columbian and modern times to further explore the notion of life and death and their interdependence.

While working on the mural at La Raza Hospital in Mexico City, Rivera and Kahlo wrote to the Communist Party to reapply for admittance. Rivera was not admitted, due to the inflexibility of the officers of the party who resented his disobedience to its policies. Kahlo, on the other hand, was allowed to join and continued her allegiance until her death. In her diary, she revealed her faith in the Communist Party and the pillars of the communist world, such as Marx, Engels, Lenin, and Mao Tse-tung.

Rivera would continue to apply for his readmittance into the Communist Party until he was finally accepted again shortly before his death.

While Rivera was completing the mural in La Raza Hospital, Kahlo had her first and only solo art exhibit at Lola Alvarez Bravo's Gallery of Contemporary Art in Mexico City. She sent out invitations, which read,

> With friendship and love born from the heart I have pleasure of inviting you to my humble exhibition. At eight in the evening—since, after all, you have a watch—I'll wait for you in the gallery of that Lola Alvarez Bravo. These paintings I painted with my own hands and they wait on the walls to give pleasure to my brothers. Well, my dear *cuate*, with true friendship I thank you for this with all my heart. Frida Kahlo de Rivera.[5]

A few nights before the opening, Lola Alvarez Bravo received a phone call letting her know that Kahlo was feeling ill, but would attend the opening with one condition. Kahlo requested a bed in the gallery because her doctors insisted on putting her on bed rest. The night of the opening reception, she arrived in an ambulance. Her bed was put in the center of the gallery where friends, artists, and admirers could congratulate her on her exhibition. Some of the prominent people that attended Kahlo's opening were Dr. Atl (painter), Andrés Henestrosa (writer), Carlos Pellicer (poet), María Izquierdo (painter), Francisco Goitia (painter), and Manuel Rodríguez Lozano, to name a few. Alvarez Bravo later wrote that they "received calls from Paris, London, and from several places in the U.S.A. asking us for details about Frida's exhibition."[6] The gallery received so many viewers that they extended the exhibition one more month to accommodate the demand of Kahlo's admirers. Rivera recalled that she was pleased at the numbers of people who were honoring her, but that she said nothing all night. He later reflected that "she must have realized she was bidding good-bye to life."[7]

All of Kahlo's paintings in the exhibition were self-portraits except for one that was a portrait of Rivera. All of the paintings submitted in this series were grim and took on an "apocalyptic note."[8] The self-portraits Kahlo painted during this period show her sufferings and awareness of her closeness to death. A short time later, Kahlo was admitted to the hospital to remove part of her right leg, in which gangrene had spread. After her amputation, Kahlo became depressed and very rarely went out. Rivera hired around-the-clock care of nurses to care for her needs and a nurse by the name of Judith Ferreto became one of the closest people to Kahlo before her death. Kahlo would often be in agony and say that "many of my good friends know I've been suffering all my life, but nobody shares the suffering, not even Diego."[9]

Although Rivera was a constant fixture in Kahlo's life, he found it difficult to see her in pain and would remove himself from the home to paint and vent his sadness. When Kahlo's pain would intensify, she would cry out for Rivera and he would leave his work to come home and comfort her. Once she was calm again, he would return to his work. At times, Ferreto and Rivera sang Kahlo to sleep during her moments of great pain. Ferreto stated, "Of necessity, Frida's life and Diego's were quite separate. They kept different hours. He left for work at eight and came home late, usually after Frida had eaten supper. They slept in different parts of the house, Frida upstairs in the modern wing, Diego downstairs in a room that, suitably, gave onto the dining room. They lived together but apart."[10]

Debilitated by her countless operations, Kahlo lived most of her life on pain medication. She consumed large amounts of morphine and she would insist on always wanting more. The drugs were obtained by prescriptions, but there came a point where her consumption went beyond the prescription. When this occurred, she would call Rivera to acquire more. In one account, a friend of the family, an art critic named Raquel Tibol, stated that "once I went to see her with Lupe Marin. . . . She was completely lost. She asked me to get her an injection. I asked, 'Where am I going to get it?' She said, open that drawer. In the drawer, behind a group of Diego's drawings, was a box with thousands of vials of Demoral."[11] In order to pay for Kahlo's care and medication, Rivera began to paint one to two paintings a day using watercolors.

On July 2, 1954, Kahlo expressed to Rivera that she wanted to attend a demonstration in protest for the CIA involvement in the coup d'état against Guatemala's President Jacobo Arbenz. Arbenz was president of Guatemala from 1951 to 1954 until, with the help of the United States, he was ousted and replaced by a military *junta* ran by a man named Colonel Carlos Castillo. Disobeying doctor's orders, Kahlo, ill with pneumonia, attended the demonstration together with Rivera in the Santo Domingo Plaza, and then they walked to the Zocalo, the central plaza of Mexico City. The demonstration would be Kahlo's last public appearance. The pneumonia that she already had was exacerbated and she became violently ill.

On July 7, Kahlo celebrated her 47th birthday with her friends by her side. She wore a white cotton *Yalalag huipil* with lavender tassels and makeup, which she had not worn for some time. More than 100 guests came to celebrate with Kahlo during her birthday dinner. In the last entry of her journal she drew a black-winged angel risen into the sky and wrote her last words: "I hope the exit is joyful—and I hope never to come back—Frida."[12]

On July 12, Rivera visited Kahlo in the evening. They spoke for some time, laughing and joking. One day later, on July 13, 1954, Frida Kahlo died, of a pulmonary embolism that may have been caused by a drug overdose, in the same room where she was born. Rivera said that the day Kahlo died was the most tragic day of his life.

The morning that Kahlo died, friends and family visited her in her home before she was taken to the Palace of Fine Arts to lie in state. Rivera, shocked with grief, sat by Kahlo's side in silence the entire morning. Rivera did not believe that Kahlo had died and, according to friend Rosa Castro,

> When she was lying in state in Bellas Artes, Diego was standing with Dr. Federico Marín, Lupe's brother. I went over and said, "What's the matter, Diego?" He said, "It's just that we are not very sure that Frida is dead." Dr. Marín said, "Diego, I assure you that she is dead." Diego said, "No, but it horrifies me to think that she still has capillary action. The hairs on her skin still stand up. It horrifies me that we should bury her in this condition." Castro said, "But it's very simple. Let the doctor open her veins. If the blood doesn't flow, it's because she's dead." So they cut Frida's skin, and there was no blood.[13]

Once Rivera saw that she was not bleeding, he came to terms with the fact that he could no longer continue believing that Kahlo was alive.

The day of Kahlo's funeral, her coffin was laid on a black cloth spread on the floor surrounded by mounds of red flowers. Although the director of the National Institute of Fine Arts, Andrés Iduarte, asked Rivera to keep politics out of the ceremony, Rivera did not comply. Her coffin was draped with a red flag that contained the Communist Party hammer and sickle in the middle of a white star. The communist symbol enraged Iduarte, but Rivera did not remove the flag. Rivera told Iduarte that if he removed the flag he was going to take Kahlo's body out into the street and stand guard there. Needless to say, the flag stayed on the coffin during the entire funeral. According to Kahlo's wishes, she wanted her coffin draped with the communist flag and Rivera complied. Rivera's act helped him become reinstated into the Communist Party the following year.

While Kahlo's friends, family, and admirers paid tribute, Cristina Kahlo, Ruth and Lupe Rivera, and others, guarded her coffin. The last honor guard consisted of Rivera, Iduarte, Siqueiros, Covarrubias, Henestrosa, former president Cárdenas, and César Martino, who was a prominent agronomist and leftist politician. In the afternoon, the Mexican national anthem and the "Corrido de Cananea" were sung while Rivera, Siqueiros, Iduarte, and others lifted Kahlo's casket and carried it into the hearse, which drove down Avenida Juárez with more than 500 people following in procession to the Dolores cemetery. Once there Iduarte, Carlos Pellicer, Adelina Zendejas, and Juan Pablo Sáinz read poems and sonnets and told stories about Kahlo. As Kahlo's body was put on an automatic cart that carried her into a crematory oven, the gatherers sang "Internationale," the national anthem, and "The Young Guard," Lenin's funeral march. As Kahlo's body went into the crematory oven, the crowd began to scream and cry out. Rivera wept and began to dig his fingernails into his fist, making his hands bleed. When the crematory door opened, Kahlo's ashes came out in the shape of her body but a gust of wind blew into the room and scattered them. Rivera immediately gathered some of the ashes and put them into a box, which he saved. Rivera's dream was to mix his ashes with Kahlo's when he died, but this never occurred.[14]

Not long after Kahlo's death, Rivera's granddaughter was baptized in the blue house. In honor of Kahlo, Rivera dressed up a Judas figure with Kahlo's clothing.[15] He also put her ashes and a corset made of plaster in the cradle to symbolize the necessity of death in life. The duality of death and life was always a recurrence in Rivera's art as well as in his life. A short time later, Rivera gave the blue house to the Mexican government. The house was turned into a museum dedicated to Frida Kahlo containing all of her personal effects, including some of her paintings.

In June 1955, Rivera was diagnosed with a recurrence of cancer of the penis, which had been first diagnosed in 1952. When the cancer returned, Mexican doctors wanted to amputate, but Rivera refused. Rivera gave up the idea of remarrying and thought that it would be unfair to go into a relationship where there would be no sexual life. Nevertheless, in July 1955 he married his friend and long-time art dealer, Emma Hurtado. The ceremony was held in the Diego Rivera Gallery owned by Hurtado in Mexico City. Although Hurtado and Rivera had known each other for 10 years, they initially kept their marriage a secret, sensitive to the fact that Kahlo's death was still very fresh in the minds of many.

Soon after Rivera and Hurtado were married, Rivera was invited by the Moscow Fine Arts Academy to research contemporary art in the Soviet Union. The couple traveled to Moscow, where Soviet doctors tried to cure Rivera's cancer with cobalt treatments that were not yet available in Mexico. The cobalt treatment is a radiotherapeutic treatment that irradiates the tumors with electrons. Rivera was treated for seven months free of cost in the finest hospital in Moscow. Once he was done with his treatment, Rivera was given a physical checkup from which he came out completely clear of any cancer.

While Rivera was in the hospital recuperating from his cancer treatments, he reflected upon his life and his past experiences:

> During my long stay in bed, I thought often of Emma's kindness, tenderness, and self-sacrificing, and of how very much like Frida she was. It made me happy to feel thus brought back to Frida. Too late now I realized that the most wonderful part of my life had been my love for Frida. But I could not really say that, given "another chance," I would have behaved toward her any differently

than I had. Every man is the product of the social atmosphere in which he grows up and I am what I am. And what sort of man was I? I had never had any morals at all and had lived only for pleasure where I found it. I was not good. I could discern other people's weaknesses easily; especially men's and then I would play upon them for no worthwhile reason. If I loved a woman, the more I loved her, the more I wanted to hurt her. Frida was only the most obvious victim of this disgusting trait. . . . As I lay in the hospital, I tried to sum up the meaning of my life, it occurred to me that I had never experienced what is commonly called "happiness." For me, "happiness" has always had a banal sound, like inspiration. Both "happiness" and "inspiration" are the words of amateurs.[16]

Rivera was eventually released from the hospital, feeling in good health, and in March 1956, Rivera and Hurtado traveled to Prague. While there he painted the image titled *Parade in Moscow*. The painting is oil on canvas and portrays a parade of Russians holding banners while a large ball is raised by the people. The large ball has the word peace written in various languages. The hammer and sickle image is depicted on a banner that symbolizes the triumph of the October Revolution. Rivera also traveled to Poland and Eastern Germany, where he painted and sketched many images such as *Hitler's Bunker Ruins of Berlin's Chancellery* and *Containing the Ice on the Danube*. These images were both painted with oil colors and portrayed scenes of Europe in this particular postwar period. All of these sketches and paintings were later displayed in the exhibition at his wife's Galería Diego Rivera. The exhibition was made up of many sketches, oils, and watercolors that focused on the discovery of the communistic world in Europe. Rivera's work was met with little reaction from the critics.

In September 1957, Rivera, now aged 70, suffered a blood clot and an attack of phlebitis that left him unable to move his right arm. During this time his heart became weak and his health became seriously endangered. On November 24, he rang a bell that he had by his bedside to call Hurtado and asked her if she could lower his bed. These were the last words Diego Rivera spoke before a heart attack took his life.

The next morning a mold of his right arm and his face was taken for a remembrance. Rivera's body was dressed in a black suit and taken

Diego Rivera in Moscow, 1955. (AP Photo)

to the rotunda of the Palace of Fine Arts. Former President Cárdenas, Dr. Atl, and David Alfaro Siqueiros stood near Rivera's body on guard. Thousands of people stood outside the palace and marched in Rivera's funeral procession. Members of the Communist Party and the Mexican government gave speeches remembering Rivera, and poet Carlos Pellicer gave the last farewell as Rivera's body was cremated.

In Rivera's will, he asked that his ashes be placed with Frida Kahlo's ashes, but Mexican President Adolfo Ruiz Cortines had prearranged for the urn to be placed in the *Rotonda de los Hombres Ilustres* in Dolores Cemetery in Mexico City. In an interview with the press, Emma Hurtado declared that the estate of Diego Rivera was worth 20 million pesos at the time of his death.

Many people have written about Rivera, about his art, his life, and his love of women, but only Frida Kahlo knew Diego Rivera in the most intimate way. She once stated,

Tomb of Diego Rivera at Dolores Cemetery, Mexico City, 1957. (Photo by Manuel Aguilar Moreno)

> I warn you that in this picture I am painting of Diego there will be colors which even I am not fully acquainted with. Besides, I love Diego so much I cannot be an objective spectator of him or his life. . . . I cannot speak of Diego as my husband because that term, when applied to him, is an absurdity. He never has been, nor will he ever be, anybody's husband. I also cannot speak of him as my lover because to me, he transcends by far the domain of sex. And if I attempt to speak of him purely, as a soul, I shall only end up by painting my own emotions. Yet considering these obstacles of sentiment, I shall try to sketch his image to the best of my ability. . . . I suppose everyone expects me to give a very feminine report about him, full of derogatory gossip and indecent revelations. Perhaps it is expected that I should lament about how I have suffered living with a man like Diego. But I do not think that the banks of a river suffer because they let the river flow, nor does the earth suffer because of the rains, nor does the atom suffer for letting its energy escape. To my way of thinking, everything has its natural compensation.[17]

These words of Frida Kahlo provide an approach to the complex life of Diego Rivera. His life was a journey between reality and myth, but one thing is certain and that is that, with his death, the world lost one of the most brilliant artists of the 20th century.

NOTES

1. Diego Rivera, *My Art, My Life* (New York: Dover Publication, 1960), 172.

2. Manuel Aguilar, *Handbook to Life in the Aztec World* (New York: Oxford University Press, 2007).

3. Anderson and Dibble, *Florentine Codex* (Santa Fe: School of American Research, 1950), 1:4.

4. Ibid., 5.

5. Ibid., 406.

6. Ibid., 409.

7. Diego Rivera with Gladys March, *My Art, My Life: An Autobiography* (New York: Dover, 1991), 177.

8. Ibid., 398.

9. Hayden Herrera, *Frida: A Biography of Frida Kahlo* (New York: First Perennial Library, 2002), 401.

10. Ibid., 402.

11. Ibid., 424.

12. Ibid., 431.

13. Herrera, *Frida*, 434.

14. Ibid., 438.

15. The Judas figures are effigies of politicians, devils, or unpopular personages made with paper mache and gun powder, which are exploded in spectacular fashion during Easter. They symbolize Judas himself, and are symbolically killed for being evildoers, traitors, thieves, or liars. Diego and Frida used to collect Judas images as pieces of folk art.

16. Rivera, *My Art, My Life*, 180.

17. Ibid., 189.

BIBLIOGRAPHY

Aguilar, Manuel-Moreno. *Handbook to Life in the Aztec World*. New York: Facts on File, 2006.

Alcántara, Isabel, and Sandra Egnolff. *Frida Kahlo and Diego Rivera*. Munich: Prestel Verlag, 1999.

Brown, Betty Ann. "The Past Idealized: Diego Rivera's Use of Pre-Columbian Imagery." In *Diego Rivera: A Retrospective*, ed. Cynthia Newman Helms. Detroit: Detroit Institute of Arts Founders Society, 1986. 139–155. Published in association with W. W. Norton, New York.

Charlot, Jean. "Diego Rivera at the Academy of San Carlos." *College Art Journal* 10 (Autumn 1950): 10–17.

Chilvers, Ian, and Harold Osborne. *The Oxford Dictionary of Art*. New York: Oxford, 1988.

Cockcroft, James. *Hispanics of Achievement: Diego Rivera*. New York: Chelsea House, 1991.

Conde, Teresa del. *Frida Kahlo: La Pintora y El Mito*. México: Instituto de Investigaciones Estéticas, Universidad Nacional Autónoma de México, 1992.

Couch, Christopher N.C. *Faces of Eternity: Masks of the Pre-Columbian Americas*. New York: Americas Society, 1991.

Craven, David. *Diego Rivera: As Epic Modernist*. New York: Prentice Hall International, 1997.

Diaz del Castillo, Bernal. *The True History of the Conquest of Mexico*. New York: McBride, 1938.

Downs, Linda Bank. *Diego Rivera: The Detroit Industry Murals*. Detroit: The Detroit Institute of Arts Founders Society, 1999.

Favela, Ramón. *Diego Rivera: The Cubist Years*. Phoenix, AZ: Phoenix Art Museum, 1984.

Fletcher, Valerie. *Crosscurrents of Modernism: Four Latin American Pioneers*. Washington, DC: Smithsonian Institution Press, 1992.

Hamill, Pete. *Diego Rivera*. New York: Abrams, 2002.

Herrera, Hayden. *Frida: A Biography of Frida Kahlo*. New York: Perennial, 2002.

Hurlburt, Laurence. *The Mexican Muralists in the United States*. Albuquerque: University of New Mexico Press, 1989.

Joseph, Emily. "'Rivera Murals in San Francisco." *Creative Art*, May 1931.

Kettenmann, Andrea. *Diego Rivera 1886–1957: Un Espíritu Revolucionario en El Arte Moderno*. Köln: Taschen, 1997.

Lee, Anthony W. *Painting on the Left: Diego Rivera, Radical Politics, and San Francisco's Public Murals*. Berkeley: University of California Press, 1999.

Marnham, Patrick. *Dreaming with His Eyes Open: A Life of Diego Rivera*. Berkeley: University of California Press, 2000.

Martínez, María Antonia. *El despegue constructivo de la Revolución. Sociedad y Política*. Mexico: Ciesas-Porrúa, 2004.

McMeekin, Dorothy. *Diego Rivera: Science and Creativity in the Detroit Murals*. Michigan: Michigan State University Press, 1985.

Petersen, Patricia. *Voladores*. Columbus, OH: Peter Bedrick Books, 2002.

Rivera, Diego (with Gladys March). *My Art, My Life: An Autobiography*. New York: Dover, 1991.

Rochfort, Desmond. *Mexican Muralists: Orozco, Rivera and Siqueiros*. San Francisco: Chronicle Books, 1993.

Rodríguez, Antonio. *A History of Mexican Mural Painting*. London: Thames and Hudson, 1969.

Taracena, Berta. *Diego Rivera: Su Obra Mural en la Ciudad de Mexico.* Mexico, D.F.: Galería de Arte Misrachi, 1981.

Torriente, Loló de la. *Memoria y Razón de Diego Rivera.* Mexico: Editorial Renacimiento, 1959.

Trotsky, Leon. "Literature and Revolution." In *Art in Theory 1900–1990: An Anthology of Changing Ideas,* ed. Charles Harrison and Paul Wood. London: Blackwell, 1992. 427.

Valentiner, William. Letter to Rivera dated April 27, 1931. Detroit Institute of Art Archives, 1931.

Weston, Edward. *The Daybooks of Edward Weston.* Millerton, NY: An Aperture Book, 1961. 1:198–99.

Wolfe, Bertram D. *The Fabulous Life of Diego Rivera.* New York: Stein & Day, 1963.

INDEX

About the Authors

MANUEL AGUILAR-MORENO is a professor of art history at California State University, Los Angeles. Dr. Aguilar-Moreno has written *Handbook of Life in the Aztec World* and *Utopia de Piedra: El Arte Tequitqui de Mexico*. He obtained the 2009 Outstanding Professor Award at Cal State LA.

ERIKA CABRERA is an art historian who combines a career as teacher and gallery curator in Los Angeles, California.